SINGAPORE'S
FISCAL STRATEGIES
FOR GROWTH
A Journey of Self-Reliance

SINGAPORE'S
FISCAL STRATEGIES
FOR GROWTH
A Journey of Self-Reliance

KOK FATT LEE
Future-Moves Group, Singapore

World Scientific

EW JERSEY · LONDON · SINGAPORE · BEIJING · SHANGHAI · HONG KONG · TAIPEI · CHENNAI · TOKYO

Published by

World Scientific Publishing Co. Pte. Ltd.

5 Toh Tuck Link, Singapore 596224

USA office: 27 Warren Street, Suite 401-402, Hackensack, NJ 07601

UK office: 57 Shelton Street, Covent Garden, London WC2H 9HE

Library of Congress Cataloging-in-Publication Data

Names: Lee, Kok Fatt, author.

Title: Singapore's fiscal strategies for growth : a journey of self-reliance /
    Kok Fatt Lee (Future-Moves Group, Singapore).

Description: New Jersey : World Scientific, [2017] | Includes bibliographical references.

Identifiers: LCCN 2017045436 | ISBN 9789813228009

Subjects: LCSH: Singapore | Fiscal policy--Singapore.

Classification: LCC HJ1361 .L425 2017 | DDC 339.5/2095957--dc23

LC record available at https://lccn.loc.gov/2017045436

British Library Cataloguing-in-Publication Data

A catalogue record for this book is available from the British Library.

For any available supplementary material, please visit
http://www.worldscientific.com/worldscibooks/10.1142/10654#t=suppl

Desk Editor: Shreya Gopi

Typeset by Stallion Press
Email: enquiries@stallionpress.com

Printed in Singapore

Endorsements

"This penetrating and comprehensive book by Lee Kok Fatt is probably the first to be written by a practitioner on Singapore's fiscal policy since the early 1960s and how that policy has contributed to the country's impressive non-inflationary and stable growth. Kok Fatt has served as the Director of Fiscal Policy in the Ministry of Finance and subsequently as the Principal Private Secretary to the President of Singapore; those two important positions have provided him with a deep and unique grasp of the factors determining the formulation and operation of the fiscal policy of Singapore. He has now compiled what may be regarded as an authoritative text book covering the diverse facets of the island state's fiscal policy. It is a valuable reference work for those, particularly students, who want to know more about an important pillar supporting Singapore's remarkable economic growth. Kok Fatt deserves praise for his stamina and dedication in completing this important oeuvre."

J Y Pillay, Chairman of the Council of Presidential Advisers

"Prudent fiscal policy has been and remains at the centre of the Singapore's success. To date, knowledge of its intricacies has been the preserve of the small handful of civil servants charged with its conduct over the last half a century. Lee Kok Fatt has done a masterful job of illuminating this vital topic for the benefit not only of the general public but also fiscal planners in Singapore and in the great number of other countries who rightly look to Singapore as an example of getting it right. This book should be a must-read for students reading up on Singapore's past success and for civil servants and politicians responsible for ensuring this success is continued."

Devadas Krishnadas, Chief Executive Officer,
Future-Moves Group and author of FUSE:
Foresight-driven Understanding, Strategy and Execution

"Many analysts have rightly attributed Singapore's success to a visionary political leadership and an effective public service well-known for their integrity, efficiency and economic orientation. In contrast, the critical role played by Singapore's fiscal policy has not received the attention that it deserves. This gap in the explanations of the Singapore story is now filled by Kok Fatt's comprehensive account of Singapore's fiscal policy as national strategy. Written in clear language that translates complex technical issues into simple terms that are easy to understand, this book is not just a useful resource but a "must-read" for anyone interested in the secrets of Singapore's success."

Professor David Chan, Director,
Behavioural Sciences Institute,
Singapore Management University and
editor of 50 Years of Social Issues in Singapore

"This is an important, readable and lively book. Many developing countries have sought to emulate Singapore's remarkable success, but until now a clear and convincing account of the decisive role of fiscal policy in that story has been lacking. The author, a former Director of Fiscal Policy at Singapore's Ministry of Finance, has deftly remedied that omission, offering insights that development practitioners, government officials and scholars everywhere should study in detail."

Max Everest-Phillips
Director, UNDP Global Centre for Public Service Excellence

Contents

Preface

When Singapore became independent in 1965, the majority of the Singapore population then lived in slums in the city or "attap" houses in the rural areas with little direct access to proper sanitation facilities and public utilities. Life expectancy at birth was 64.5 years. Annual average unemployment was 9.2%[1] and expected to get worse as post World War II baby boomers entered the workforce. The economy, which comprised mainly commerce and trade services tied to Singapore's *entrepôt* activities, was not able to grow quickly enough to create jobs for the growing population.

Singapore had lost a large hinterland when it left Malaysia just 2 years after joining the federation. Communism was at the doorstep to the region as newly independent countries sought to find a new way forward. Many observers did not expect Singapore to survive, much less prosper as a nation. A small island made up largely of granite rock, Singapore has few other natural resources besides the surrounding deep waters which makes it suitable as a port. Fast forwarding 52 years, this little piece of rock is now among the most prosperous nations in the world. Singapore has become one of the busiest transhipment ports in the world, handling more than half a million tonnes in sea cargo and more than 30 million twenty-foot equivalent units (TEUs) in container throughput. It is also an aviation hub, with its airports handling more than 1.8 million tonnes in air cargo.[2]

Remarkably for a small city state with little natural resources, Singapore has one of the largest sovereign wealth funds in the world, providing the backing to a strong and stable Singapore dollar and generating a stream of investment income that helps the Singapore government keep taxes low.

Besides being a global manufacturing and financial centre, Singapore is one of the world's most liveable cities. More than 90% of resident households own their homes. This is among the highest home ownership rates in the world. Life expectancy has risen to around 82 years, the remarkable improvement attributed to better living conditions and improved health services as the nation grew wealthier. According to the Mercer Quality of Living Study 2017, Singapore has the world's best infrastructure.

This book explicates how fiscal strategies adopted in Singapore have uniquely contributed to the country's sustained growth and the lessons that can be drawn for governance. When Singapore commemorated its 50th year of independence in 2015, many observers ascribed the island state's achievements to several factors such as its strategic location in the region, a hardworking population, sound policies and a stable political environment. It went from a Third World to a First World country in just one generation. But as many commentators pointed out, the nation has been experiencing "first world" problems in more recent years. A rapidly ageing population raises concerns over the adequacy of savings for retirement and the ability of the economy to support higher healthcare spending. Some — both analysts and ordinary Singaporeans — questioned the need for the economy to continue growing as fast as before as infrastructure strained to accommodate a growing foreign workforce to drive economic growth. In an increasingly interconnected world, where the winner takes all and technology is making many low and middle-income jobs obsolete, more Singaporeans are increasingly concerned over the increasing income gap.

The world is now facing many challenges. In the aftermath of the Global Financial Crisis, growth in developed economies has slowed, especially in the US and Europe, which had been the engines of global growth since the last world war. Emerging economies have picked up some of the slack but they face many constraints in maintaining their growth momentum. The challenges of an ageing population, global growth slowdown and technological disruption affect not only Singapore but also many other nations and cities around the world. Adequate policy action, including in the area of fiscal policy, is needed to sustain global growth. Many Singaporeans worried if they could continue to enjoy the growth and prosperity that their parents and grandparents had experienced in Singapore's first 50 years. Parents have similar worries for the prospects of their children.

When I was Director of Fiscal Policy in the Singapore Ministry of Finance from 2007 to 2011, I received frequent requests to brief pre-university and undergraduate students, as well as colleagues from other parts of the Civil Service on Singapore's fiscal policies. The Ministry of Finance also regularly received foreign government delegations who were interested to know how Singapore's fiscal policies worked. There is no complete textbook on Singapore's fiscal strategies yet, though much has been written on the technical workings of specific aspects of Singapore's fiscal policy from the perspectives of academics and other experts. Drawing on their work as well as policy statements by the Singapore government, I attempt to present in this book a non-technical but holistic view of Singapore's fiscal policy including how the different elements interrelate and work together as a functioning system and also the system's impact and implications.

I hope this book can be useful as a reference material not only for students and public officials, but also for anyone who is interested to learn about the workings of Singapore's fiscal policy. A better understanding of Singapore's fiscal system and strategies would contribute to better-informed discourses and deliberations on the policy options for sustainable growth in Singapore as well as other countries. Certainly, what worked in Singapore may not work in other countries. But just as Singapore has always learned and adapted (rather than fully adopted) from systems in other countries in its development, perhaps Singapore's fiscal system can provide a useful case study for other countries to examine and extract lessons or implications.

While the pioneer generation leaders of the Singapore Ministry of Finance, including Dr Goh Keng Swee, Mr Hon Sui Sen, Mr J Y

Pillay, Mr Sim Kee Boon and Mr Ngiam Tong Dow established the foundations on which Singapore's fiscal policies developed, subsequent generations of Finance Ministry Officials have built on and fine-tuned the policies over time as Singapore developed. I had the privilege of working with some of them, such as Mr Lim Siong Guan, Mr Teo Ming Kian, Mr Peter Ong, Mr Lim Hup Seng, Mr Donald Low, Ms Jacqueline Poh, Mr Derrick Wan and Mr Ng Wai Choong. This book is dedicated to them. I would also like to express my gratitude to mentors and friends such as Mr J Y Pillay, Professor David Chan, Mr Devadas Krishnadas, Mr Max Everest-Phillips, Mrs Belinda Tay and Mr Tamil Selven who generously offered much valued advice and encouragement when I was working on this book.

About the Author

Mr Lee Kok Fatt is currently Director at the Future-Moves Group, a strategic management consultancy based in Singapore. Prior to joining the company, Kok Fatt served in the Singapore Civil Service for two decades, during which he held senior positions such as Principal Private Secretary (PPS) to the Singapore President, and Director (Fiscal Policy) at the Ministry of Finance.

Kok Fatt was a Sloan Fellow at the London Business School where he read for a Masters in Management. He also holds a Bachelors of Accounting (First Class) from Nanyang Technological University (NTU). He was awarded the Public Administration (Silver) Medal by the President of the Republic of Singapore in 2016.

SECTION I

INTRODUCTION

Chapter 1

Much More than a Revenue and Expenditure Statement

Most people think of the term "fiscal policy" as the annual government budget, which is essentially a listing of the government's expenditure plan for the financial year stating how much the government plans to spend and where the spending would be made, such as in defence, education, healthcare, infrastructure, and industrial development.

In some countries, the government presents a multi-year budget, providing more information on how expenditures could vary over the years in tandem with implementation of government programmes. For example, if the spending plans were to involve the development of infrastructure, the developmental expenditure may start off at a lower level and ramp up over the period as construction takes place.

The annual budget also lays out how the government plans to finance the expenditures. The financing plan usually includes the raising of revenues through a combination of different types of taxes and fees and charges on services or concessions provided by the government. Government revenues may also include the sale of state-owned assets including natural resources such as crude oil or land, physical properties such as buildings and infrastructure, or state-operated businesses like ports or airports. The levels of the taxes, fees and charges, and other revenues vary from country to country depending on several factors, such as economic development and social needs. The levels of the revenues could also vary over time based on projected or assumed economic growth rates, inflation, changes to the rates of taxes, and collections of fees and charges. When revenues are insufficient to finance the expenditures, deficits occur and the plans would usually also lay out how the shortfalls would be met. This could involve borrowing which should be accompanied by plans regarding how the borrowings would be paid back, such as by increasing revenues or cutting expenditures in the future.

Beyond the top lines of revenue and expenditures, the government's fiscal strategies reflect the nation's current and future priorities. The annual budget usually attracts broad-based attention because it reflects the government's longer-term strategies affecting all stakeholders (e.g., citizens, local and foreign investors, and immigrant workers) directly or indirectly. For example, how much the government decides to spend in public services would affect the level and types of services the public would enjoy. Payments by the government to suppliers and wages paid to civil servants add to domestic consumption, which boosts the economy. The government may also make social welfare transfers to the lower income or unemployed in accordance with the social compact. The level of taxes and the types of taxes implemented will in turn affect investment and consumption decisions. For example, raising government revenues by increasing taxes on incomes reduces profits of businesses. Taxes imposed on expenditures on goods and services raise prices for consumers. If the government fails to raise enough revenues to pay for its spending, it will incur debts that need to be paid off eventually by cutting down on spending or collecting higher government revenues in the future. Taking together the different effects, the impact of the budget on the well-being of the people is pervasive and enduring. Therefore, the government's fiscal strategies are much more than a revenue and expenditure statement.

In Singapore's case, fiscal strategies serve to support economic and social policies. They also facilitate the conduct of monetary policy by the Monetary Authority of Singapore to promote non-inflationary economic growth. Therefore, I have also dedicated some parts of this book to describing these policies to set the context in which Singapore's fiscal strategies operate.

Chapter 2

Historical Developments

Celebrating in 2017 its 52nd year of independence, Singapore is still a young nation by many yardsticks. But its development as a modern economy began much earlier in the 18th century when it was established as a British trading outpost in 1819.

Policy options are determined by the developments and choices made in history. To appreciate Singapore's fiscal strategies, one has to understand the historical context of the country's policy development. Singapore has, for most part of its history, been a city, providing services to its geographical region and beyond. By a twist of fate, the city became a state half a century ago, in 1965. As a small city state without a hinterland, Singapore did not have much strategic room to manoeuvre but had to continue being a hub connected to the global flow of goods, capital, and people.

Pre-Independence Growth

In 1819, Singapore was discovered by the British who found the island, strategically located along the Straits of Malacca with a natural deep water harbour, an ideal transhipment port to support the British trade in spices with the Far East. The later development of the rubber and tin industries in neighbouring Malaysia further boosted economic activities in Singapore, which supported the trading of these

7

commodities and their export to the rest of the world. No taxes were imposed on the import and export of goods, which was a novel approach to run a port at that time. The port was sustained by fees paid by shippers for the port services. Ancillary commercial activities such as banking, trading, and other domestic services also attracted businessmen and workers from around the region and beyond.

Singapore was a made a Crown Colony of the British Empire in 1867, after which much of the foundation for the governance of Singapore was built based on British administrative and legal systems. Commercial capabilities to support the shipping and commercial activities, including an exchange rate system pegged to the Sterling, were also established. Up until the 1960s, Singapore operated a *laissez faire* system which allowed the free flow of capital, goods, and people into and out of Singapore.[3]

Post-Independence Challenges

Singapore was granted self-government by the British in 1959 and subsequently became part of the Federation of Malaysia in 1963. When it eventually separated from Malaysia in 1965, it lost access to a hinterland, the common market with Malaysia. Singapore's problems were exacerbated by the withdrawal of British troops in 1971. The total expenditures of the British armed forces comprised a substantial 16% of gross domestic product (GDP) in 1966. Some 31,500 locally enlisted personnel and locally recruited civilians worked in the British bases.[4]

When the People's Action Party (PAP) won the first local elections to form the first local government in 1959, one of its first challenges was to provide jobs for a young and growing population. Unemployment was estimated by some to be as high as 13.5% and could get worse because despite Singapore's capabilities in commerce and trade, these sectors alone would not be able to generate the growth in income and jobs needed to support the young and growing population. Besides unemployment, the poor infrastructure and social services needed urgent improvement. However, the government faced a budget deficit estimated to be about $42 million (then around 1.5% of GDP) and reserves were low.[5]

As a small city state with no natural resources, Singapore could not engage in the import-substitution policies undertaken by larger developing countries to grow its manufacturing sector. The small domestic market of Singapore's population, which was then less than two million, limited the types of products that could be produced at equivalent cost to imports. Singapore therefore made a bold decision to develop a manufacturing sector that produced for the regional and global markets instead of its domestic market. It was an act of faith for several reasons. First, unlike in South Korea and Hong Kong, there was a lack of local industrialists in Singapore. Second, the infrastructure to support a manufacturing sector was lacking. Third, domestic savings were low and banks were not prepared to provide loans to support local manufacturing activities.

Fortunately for Singapore, multinational corporations (MNCs) in developed countries were looking to move manufacturing activities out of their home markets where costs were rising. The MNCs provided the global talent and capital that Singapore needed to jumpstart its industrialisation efforts. Besides allowing Singapore to overcome the lack of industrial capabilities among the locals, the MNCs had the financial capital, technology as well as large, growing home markets to which the goods could be exported. This enabled Singapore to bypass regional markets which were then at the stage of growing their industries and protecting their own markets.

Singapore began a major endeavour to build the infrastructure needed to host the manufacturing bases of MNCs to kick-start the goods export sector. Among the infrastructural projects, the most ambitious — or some would say audacious — involved the reclamation of a swamp in the western part of Singapore to create a large contiguous greenfield area on which roads, wharfs, electrical grids, water pipes, and whatever else needed to support the factories would be built. It was clearly a risky decision because it was by no means certain that the MNCs would come to Singapore. At one point, the project was called "Goh's folly", a jibe at Dr Goh Keng Swee,

Singapore's Minister for Finance from 1959 to 1965, who initiated the project.[6]

The critics were eventually proven wrong. Dr Goh and his team succeeded in their endeavours to attract MNCs to set up their manufacturing operations at the industrial parks when they were built. Unlike many other countries that gained independence from the British colonial masters, Singapore did not have any hang-ups about welcoming the foreign investors of the West to Singapore's shores. In fact, Singapore maintained the governance systems that the British had built up over the years, which given the similarity to the systems of the West, helped in attracting foreign investment.

Taxes were also kept low to encourage business investments needed to jump-start the industrialisation effort. Dr Goh granted "pioneer status" to the investors, which significantly reduced the taxes to be paid by the MNCs. Labour laws were also tightened to effectively disallow union interference with management decisions regarding recruitment, promotion and deployment, and provided for negotiation of longer-term agreements, to give clarity to the ambit of unions. This reduced the number of strikes and improved labour productivity significantly for employers. All these factors, which made Singapore an ideal location as a manufacturing base for MNCs, contributed to the birth of the goods export sector, which was to drive Singapore's growth over the next half a century.

Chapter 3

Building a Sustainable Budget from the Beginning

When the British granted self-government to Singapore, the colonial masters effectively ceded all executive control (except security and foreign affairs) to the first Singapore government formed by PAP in 1959. PAP eventually led Singapore to join the Federation of Malaysia in 1963, marking the end of British rule in Singapore. However, Singapore's merger with Malaysia was fraught with difficulties due to competition and conflicts in various areas ranging from economic and financial issues to the fundamental political question of Malaysia's national identity.[7] Two years later, Singapore left the Malaysian Federation and became a sovereign nation.

There were many competing needs in Singapore's early difficult years as an independent nation. The PAP government decided that it was most important to address the worsening unemployment problem and improve social services for its population. Consequently, PAP released the First State Development Plan (1961–1965), costing around $870 million (current dollars) in 1961, to develop the social and economic infrastructure to improve the well-being of the Singapore people. The plan included the development of an island-wide public utilities (water and electricity) infrastructure, public housing programme to improve living conditions of the general population, and industrial facilities to support the development of the manufacturing sector.

The building of the social and economic infrastructure under the First State Development Plan[8] was to be financed in part (around $360 million or 40% of the expenditures under the plan) by government surpluses, sale of government assets and other reserve funds belonging to statutory boards such as the City Council Consolidated Rate Fund, Public Utility Departments of the City Council, and Singapore Harbour Board Reserve Fund. The other $500 million or 57% would be financed by loans. A substantial part of the loans required would be raised from internal sources through subscription to government loans of about $230 million by the public and public sector agencies, with the balance of about $271 million from foreign sources such as the World Bank and the UK government.[a]

The investments into power, water, gas, housing, and industrial development were expected to yield additional revenues and be "bankable", that is, the projects would pay for themselves with some rates of return. Incidentally, 58% of the expenditures under the development plan was allocated for economic development,[9] slightly more than the 57% that was raised from loans. It would be reasonable to expect that the value created by economic growth generated by the plan would yield the fiscal resources to repay the loans. Indeed, while the projects led to government budget deficits[b] for the most part of the 1960s, the government managed to turn in budget surpluses every year from 1968 onwards, except in 1987, following Singapore's first recession.[10]

Self-Sufficiency in Operations

A Development Fund was created by legislation in 1953 to allow financial resources to be accumulated for lumpy development

---

[a] The UK Government provided a grant of $8.6 million to make up the balance.
[b] Deficit/surplus as defined by IMF as Total Revenue (Total Revenue + Grant) – Total Expenditure (Total Expenditure + Lending – Repayments).

expenditures. The government may make transfers of financial resources from its operating revenues into the Development Fund to finance development plans.

The Development Fund was retained by the PAP government when Singapore gained self-government status in 1959. In addition to injections from operating revenues, the Development Fund was used to hold the borrowings undertaken by the government for the First State Development Plan. The Fund could only be tapped on for the government's direct development expenditure for the construction, improvement, acquisition or replacement of capital assets and land acquisition. The Development Fund Act was amended in 1959 to allow the Development Fund to make grants and loans to, or investments in, any public agency or corporation for the development projects. The repayments of any loans made from the fund or payments of interest on such loans, and the interest and income from investments of the fund and profits arising from realisation of any such investments, would go back to the Development Fund.

Consequently, the funds raised from external and domestic loans were lent through the Development Fund to public sector agencies created to administer development projects under the First State Development Plan. The Housing Development Board (HDB) was created to build HDB flats to house people who were relocated from squatter slums. The Public Utilities Board (PUB) was instituted to develop the infrastructure to supply drinking water and electricity to households and businesses. The Economic Planning Unit (subsequently reconstituted as the Economic Development Board or EDB), oversaw the development of industrial parks, the largest of which involved reclaiming a swamp land in the western part of Singapore (Jurong), supported by a port and accommodation for workers. The Jurong Town Corporation (JTC) was later constituted to take over from EDB the role of industrial facilities development and management.

These agencies were tasked with collection of fees and charges from the users of the infrastructure to finance and repay the loans back to the government. The first HDB flats were let out on rental basis to generate revenues that would enable HDB to finance loans taken out from the government for building the flats. Subsequently, Singaporeans could purchase them using their savings under the Central Provident Fund (CPF),[c] with subsidies from the government that were paid to HDB so that it continued to recover the full development costs of the HDB flats. PUB ensured that water and electricity were supplied at charges that recovered the costs of production of the utilities. Industrial lands were leased out by EDB (and later JTC) at cost recovery rates to companies for building of factories.

In this way, Singapore's first Finance Minister Dr Goh Keng Swee imposed the principle of self-sufficiency by ensuring that borrowings were only to be used for development purposes. On the other hand, the agencies were tasked to ensure that the loans taken could be recovered with interest for repayment. In addition, the government's recurrent expenditures had to be financed from taxes, fees, and charges collected by the government. In fact, Dr Goh set the tone in 1959, when he was appointed the Finance Minister. He undertook austerity measures to bring an expected budget deficit of about $42 million (about 1.5% GDP[d]), to balance through various austerity measures including the reduction of civil servant benefits and bonuses, and streamlining and the reprioritisation of public sector projects.[11]

Ensuring Self-Reliance in Funding

As a new nation, Singapore did not settle on the easy option of foreign aid, which risked creating a sense of dependency on the charity of foreign-aid givers. Instead, to nurture a self-reliant culture, the government opted to raise funds domestically in the first instance. But

---

[c] CPF was set up as a pension plan in 1955 by the colonial government to provide social security for the working population in Singapore. The scheme required contributions of a certain percentage of the individual employee's monthly salary toward the employee's personal and portable account in the fund by both employers and employees, respectively.

[d] GDP in nominal dollars was $2.9 billion in 1959.

due to the insufficiency of local savings, the government had to access foreign loans. In that event, Singapore chose to borrow from multilateral development banks, which helped instil the discipline of ensuring that the loans go towards credit worthy projects.

Thus, Singapore's Development Fund initially comprised domestic and external loans raised by the government and supplemented by government revenues. External loans comprised borrowings from the UK government, World Bank and Asian Development Bank which were used to finance projects that supported economic development. External loans peaked in 1978 at more than $1 billion before steadily declining to nil in 1995.

To reduce the reliance on external loans for Singapore's developmental needs, the government sought to raise domestic savings through the CPF scheme. Under the CPF scheme, all employers and employees were required to contribute 5% of the monthly salary on each side to the employees' CPF accounts, which could only be withdrawn by the employee on retirement at age 55. The constitution of the CPF Board required that the funds be invested for a return. From 1959, the CPF Board invested in government bonds which provided a safe form of investment that yielded the required returns on CPF savings.[12] Subsequently, the government raised CPF rates in phases from 5% on each side (employees and employers) in 1968 to 10% in 1971. The savings in CPF grew from about $47 million in 1965 to $224 million in 1971 because of the rapid growth in employment as well as the increase in contribution rates.[13]

Beside the CPF, the Post Office Savings Bank (POSB) and other public sector entities also held government securities. The Monetary Authority of Singapore (MAS) was empowered by the Development Loan Act to undertake the issue and management of government securities on behalf of the government. Proceeds of such loans raised were required to be paid into the Development Fund and applied to the purposes of the Fund.

The deployment of the domestic savings towards financing of infrastructure projects enabled the large-scale development projects to be implemented without inflation. During the period from 1965 to 1970, the prime lending rate among banks was 8%.[14] If the government had borrowed such a large amount from the banks, this would have drained liquidity from the banks and jacked up interest rates beyond the 8%. The higher interest rates would have affected domestic private consumption and investment. On the other hand, by utilising the CPF savings, the government only had to pay a spread over the 2.5% that the CPF had to pay to the CPF members on the savings accounts. The higher domestic private savings rate allowed the government to borrow from domestic sources at relatively stable and low interest rates for development of infrastructure at lower costs.

As the fiscal situation improved, the need to borrow for funding of development expenditure diminished. In addition, statutory boards such as HDB and JTC were encouraged to tap the capital markets in Singapore directly to fund their development expenditures. The government therefore no longer needed to borrow to fund even its development expenditures.

Keeping Costs Low for Investors

Low Direct Taxes

To raise revenues for financing of the expected increase in expenditures, tax increases were spread out among different forms of taxes, fees and charges, such as duties on liquid petroleum gas, levy on telephone and utility bills, and stamp duties on transfers of motor vehicles. This reduced the need for a large increase in income tax rates which would have a negative drag on investments needed to grow the economy.[15]

To encourage private investments in manufacturing, tax incentives for business investments were announced.[16] This included the provision of pioneer tax status offering reduced tax rates for the first few years of manufacturing operation and accelerated depreciation allowances on investments, which further lowered the taxes that were to be paid by investors in the manufacturing sector that would provide jobs for the people.

Land Acquisition to Redeploy Land towards Productive Activities

Through a national land acquisition exercise, state ownership of land was raised from 44% in 1960 to 76% by 1985. The Land Acquisition Act (enacted in 1966) enabled acquisition of land based on values that reflected current use^c, a large part of which was then rural land. This kept the cost of land low and allowed the various agencies such as JTC and HDB to recover the land cost of their infrastructure by charging rates that were acceptable to their users. As the major owner of land, the government could plan for the development of social and economic infrastructure in an optimal and cost efficient way.[17]

Foundations for a Sustainable Budget

The series of major and interrelated government decisions taken in the early days of Singapore's independence, as briefly summarised in this chapter, constituted the foundational factors for building a sustainable budget from the beginning. Promoting budgetary self-sufficiency in operations, self-reliance in funding of development projects, and keeping overall costs low to encourage business investments — these continued to be the fundamental tenets of Singapore's fiscal policy framework over the years since independence.

---

^cBetween 1973 and 1987, compensation was pegged at the market value of the land as of 30 November 1973 or the date of acquisition, whichever was lower. Compensation has been pegged at current market rates from 1987.

Chapter 4

Evolution of Growth Strategies over the Years

Continuation of Growth Strategy into the 70s and 80s

By the early 1970s, the problem of unemployment was effectively solved. The government then shifted its focus to encouraging the setting up of more capital intensive and higher value-add industries that required the use of trained and skilled workers who would earn higher incomes.

Complementing this shift, the government invested into technical education by establishing vocational institutes and technical secondary schools to increase the supply of skilled labour needed by the industries. To address the tight labour situation, the government also allowed more foreign workers, first from Malaysia and then subsequently from other countries (non-traditional sources). This strategy continued into the 1980s, when Singapore became an established manufacturing hub.[18]

The tight labour market soon resulted in upward pressures on wages. At the same time, countries developing with lower costs in the region began to embark on export-oriented growth strategies and competed with Singapore for investments from MNCs. The construction sector also declined as the demand for public housing fell after many years of robust growth. Coupled with the slowdown in global economic growth, Singapore experienced its first recession in 1985. This triggered the setting up of the Economic Committee in 1985, which was a national-level committee led by the then Minister of State for Trade and Industry Mr Lee Hsien Loong, to look into the causes of the recession. The Economic Committee traced the root cause to the fact that Singapore had become more expensive due to resource constraints and structural inefficiencies. The government's drive in the early 1980s to force an improvement in productivity by raising wages and CPF contributions rates had driven up labour costs. In short, Singapore had lost its cost competitiveness relative to other countries.

The Economic Committee made decisive recommendations for Singapore to speed up economic restructuring, including developing the services sector, upgrading industrial and business capabilities towards higher-value activities, and renewing the emphasis on raising productivity. To restore cost competitiveness, structural reforms were made to enhance wage flexibility in the labour market. Sectors with potential for growth such as banking and finance, transport and communications, and international services were liberalised. The government also made the policy U-turn of cutting the CPF rates to reduce labour costs.[19]

Investment into New Drivers of Growth

The recession in 1985 underlined Singapore's vulnerability as a small economy exporting to the world. Since then, the Singapore government has regularly reviewed its economic strategies to ensure that Singapore continues to be relevant to the world over the longer term.

In 1991, the Economic Planning Committee presented a Strategic Economic Plan (SEP)[20] charting a long-term economic course for Singapore in continuation of the work of the Economic Committee in 1985. Based on the SEP, industrial strategy was refined to develop capabilities at the ecosystem or cluster level in niche areas, such as electronics, petrochemicals, and engineering, where Singapore had developed deep expertise. The cluster approach would enable Singapore to entrench these economic activities by building on the strong synergies between interrelated firms and industries that would be difficult to replicate in other countries. Incentives were also given to encourage Singapore companies to tap on the growth of the region to overcome domestic resource and market constraints by investing abroad to develop to a "Second Wing" of the economy.

In addition, the government promoted technology development as a driver of growth. A 5-year National Technology Plan costing $2 billion was announced in 1991. At the end of the 5-year period, the budget for the next 5-year National Science and Technology Plan was doubled to $4 billion. The National Science and Computing Board was established in 1991 to foster scientific research and talent for a knowledge-based economy. To prepare Singapore for the internet revolution, the National Computer Board, which was set up in 1981 to spearhead the computerisation of the Public Service and develop the local computer services sector, was merged with the Telecommunication Authority of Singapore to form the Infocomm Development Authority (IDA) of Singapore in 1999 to master plan and develop the information communication infrastructure and sector. In 2016, IDA and the Media Development Authority of Singapore (MDA) were restructured to form the Info-communications Media Development Authority of Singapore (IMDA) and the Government Technology Agency (GovTech). The IMDA leverages on the convergence of media and telecommunications to better regulate and promote the development of the infocomm sector, while GovTech brings a sharper focus on digital transformation efforts in the public sector.

Services as the Second Engine of Growth

The Economic Review Committee (ERC) constituted in 2003 marked a milestone in Singapore's growth strategy. The ERC articulated the importance of growing as a global city and a hub of talent, enterprise, and innovation. The ERC leveraged on the idea of a global city as a driver of economic growth, by attracting creative talent from around the world to come together to create new products and services.[21]

Consequently, Singapore gave greater emphasis to promoting innovation, enterprise, and entrepreneurship. Labour policies shifted to attracting more professionals and creative talents to make Singapore a global city and a talent hub. The development of the services sector was also given more attention. To develop Singapore as a total business centre beyond a manufacturing hub, incentives that had been provided for manufacturing activities were extended to companies for investments in service sectors. Over time, as modern services developed, the services sector became the second engine of growth alongside the manufacturing sector.

Responding to Competition and Volatility in Demand

From the late 1990s to the late 2000s, Singapore was buffeted by a series of global shocks, beginning with the Asian Financial Crisis in 1997, followed by the bursting of the dot-com bubble in 2001, outbreak of severe acute respiratory syndrome (SARS) and Iraq War in 2003, and the Global Financial Crisis in 2008. This decade-long period of volatility in global demand was accompanied by the integration into the world market of Asian giants China and India, which brought considerable manufacturing capacities to the world at low cost.

Singapore had to respond to these challenges by adjusting taxes and providing fiscal support to buffer viable businesses from the global shocks, while speeding up restructuring efforts to help businesses upgrade and move into value-add activities to set themselves apart from the competition coming from regional low-cost countries. At the same time, fiscal incentives were provided to encourage businesses to internationalise and tap on the growth of new markets in China and India, as well as the region.

Shift towards Productivity-Driven Growth

Economic growth had hitherto been largely driven by the growth in capital stock and labour. From 1970 to 2014, net foreign direct investment grew from $0.3 billion to $34 billion, and the total labour force from 0.7 million to 3.5 million. The labour force increase was driven partly by an increase in labour force participation rates among the resident workforce, especially among women (which more than doubled from 28% to 59% over the same period), but immigration was the main driver of workforce growth.

However, economic growth from factor accumulation (i.e., the growth of capital and labour) has its limits. Capital stock accumulation is subject to diminishing returns to scale. Growing the economy by increasing labour inputs is also constrained by infrastructural limits and social concerns. Following the Global Financial Crisis, the Economic Strategies Committee (ESC) set up in 2010 recommended a shift from factor driven growth to driving growth across the board through productivity improvements, skills, and innovation. The committee re-emphasised the strategies to grow by becoming an innovative economy and a global city and commercialisation of research and development (R&D) to create new products and services. Recognising the limits of growing by ever-increasing labour inputs, the ESC articulated the need to limit the growth of foreign workers while continuing to welcome foreign talent. It also recognised Singapore's constraints in land and energy resources and highlighted the need to improve land productivity and build a smart energy economy.[22]

Following the ESC's recommendations, the government strengthened its pace of reforms to tighten the inflow of foreign workers by raising the Foreign Worker Levy and providing a wider slew of incentives to encourage Singaporean workers to upgrade their skills and companies to invest in innovation and productivity improvements. A 5-year research, innovation, and enterprise (RIE) plan costing $16.1 billion was announced in 2011, and this was followed up by another 5-year RIE plan costing $19 billion announced in 2015.

In October 2015, the government announced that a "Committee on the Future Economy" (CFE) would be established to develop economic strategies to position Singapore for the future. On 9 February 2017, the committee released its report outlining recommendations to keep Singapore's economy competitive by deepening and expanding existing capabilities in areas such as international connectedness and digital competencies. The committee also built on the ESC report to recommend measures to help workers acquire and utilise new skills and enable firms to innovate and raise productivity by scaling up and working together with other stakeholders to bring about transformational changes at the industry level. In the ensuing annual budget announced on 20 February 2017, the government included a $2.4 billion package to support measures to build capacities for the future economy in response to the recommendations in the CFE report as follows:

— $1 billion injection into the National Productivity Fund to support industry transformation;
— $500 million injection into the National Research Fund to support R&D activities in Singapore;
— $100 million for the SkillsFuture leadership development initiative, to groom future Singapore business leaders for enterprises going regional/global and to digitise, and the Global Innovation Alliance;
— $600 million for an International Partnership Fund to co-invest with Singapore-based firms to help them scale up and internationalise;
— $150 million for a Public Sector Construction Productivity Fund; and
— $80 million for a SME Go Digital Programme.

Summary

Singapore's economic growth strategy has been consistent in terms of ensuring that the country is plugged into the global flow of goods, people, and capital to serve the world. Through the years, the fiscal strategies adopted by Singapore have supported the country's growth by sustaining the investment of fiscal resources into the development of land, infrastructure, and manpower to build a competitive economy that continually evolves to remain relevant in a changing global market.

SECTION II

STABILITY FOR LONG-TERM GROWTH

Chapter 5

Steering a Small Ship in Rough Seas

Since independence, Singapore has enjoyed rapid growth and now has one of the highest per capita GDP in the world.[23] The markets that Singapore exports to now include the major markets in the West (the US and EU), and developing markets in Asia including China, Malaysia, and Indonesia.

But Singapore also experienced wide swings in the growth rates, which reflected global economic and geopolitical events. Despite recent efforts to diversify its economy, Singapore's exports are still affected by global cycles at the aggregate level.[24] As shown in Fig. 1, Singapore has seen increasingly large and frequent fluctuations in its growth rates even as its economy matured over the years.

After several years of good growth since independence, Singapore was buffeted by the two oil shocks in the 1970s. In 1985, Singapore suffered its first recession which was mainly due to internal factors of reduced cost competitiveness. Subsequently, Singapore experienced sharp slowdowns that reflected global events such as the Asian Financial Crisis in 1998, the bursting of the dot.com bubble in 2001, the SARS epidemic, and Iraq War in 2003. When the subprime mortgage crisis hit the world during the Global Financial Crisis at the end of 2008, Singapore was among the first countries in the world to

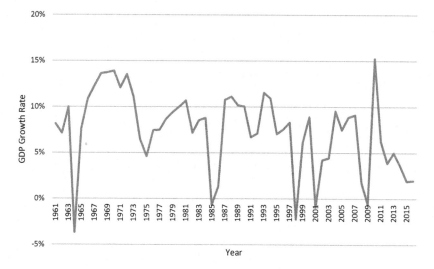

Figure 1: Singapore's Annual GDP Percentage Growth Rates at 2010 Market Prices (1961–2016).

Source: Singapore Department of Statistics

enter into a recession. In fact, Singapore has become so integrated with the rest of the world, global observers have described Singapore as the proverbial "canary in the coal mine"[25] of the world economy.

In each of the global events that impacted Singapore, the government responded swiftly with measures to not only cushion an otherwise hard landing but also steer the economy towards safer waters by restructuring and creating new capabilities in line with longer-term strategic shifts in the world. Table 1 summarises the fiscal measures undertaken by the government over the years in response to the global shocks.

Low Fiscal Multiplier in Singapore

It is noteworthy that through every downturn, the government did not engage in policies to artificially prop up aggregate demand as the main objective. For example, though the government announced the

Table 1:   Summary of Fiscal Measures in Response to Economic Downturns.[26]

Event	Policy Response
Oil Shock in the 1970s — quadrupling of oil prices leading to global inflation and economic slowdown	The government did not undertake fiscal measures to lower prices, such as by providing subsidies for certain essential goods like foodstuffs, electricity, and petrol. This would have been costly and would have obstructed the functioning of the markets. Businesses would not have had the incentives to undertake the necessary measures to adjust their consumption of such goods, and would not have restructured themselves to become more cost competitive. Rather, the government decided to focus on monetary measures as a response because the main concern was managing inflationary expectations. Policy responses included appreciation of the Singapore dollar to reduce prices of imports into Singapore and tightening of credit controls on financial institutions. The National Trade Union Congress (NTUC) also started a supermarket chain to ensure that basic foodstuffs and household items remained reasonably priced to address concerns of profiteering.
1985 — First recession as global demand weakened just as the construction sector went through a slump, and cost increases due to inflexibilities in the labour markets and other sectors weakened Singapore's competitiveness.	Fiscal measures included wage restraint for the public sector in line with Economic Committee recommendations for employers. CPF rate cuts were also announced. Tax reliefs such as increased depreciation allowance for capital expenditures were granted to boost investment. Rebates on personal, corporate, and property taxes as well as government fees were also granted. These measures helped businesses reduce costs and remain competitive in the global context. Consequently, this avoided a further loss of jobs.

(Continued)

Table 1: (*Continued*)

Event	Policy Response
1997 — Asian Financial Crisis when regional currencies collapsed leading to collapse in regional demand and business confidence. Singapore became costlier due to significant appreciation of the Singapore dollar against regional currencies. Downturn in property prices and demand in Singapore.	Fiscal measures focussed on reduction in business costs through property and corporate tax rebates and reduction in fees and charges. Wages were cut in line with National Wage Council recommendations. Cuts in CPF rates were also announced to reduce costs for employers. In addition, to avoid a collapse of the property market, the government announced property market measures such as suspension of government land sales, and measures to help property developers cope with cash flow issues by deferring taxes on uncompleted projects. To provide help for the construction sector, development projects were accelerated to soak up the fall in construction demand from property developers.
2001 — Bursting of the dot.com bubble in the US. Fall in US demand resulting in contraction of manufacturing sector in Singapore.	Fiscal measures included business cost reduction measures such as rebates in taxes and fees and charges. For households and individuals, a $3 billion cash transfer to Singaporeans (New Singapore Shares scheme) targeted at the lower-income groups was introduced. Public sector infrastructure projects brought forward to boost construction demand.
2003 — Outbreak of Severe Acute Respiratory Syndrome (SARS) epidemic, which resulted in a sharp fall in tourist arrivals. This coincided with continued weakness in global demand due to downturn in electronics and Info-communication Technology (IT) cycle. The financial markets also reacted adversely when US invaded Iraq in 2003.	A SARS Relief Package totalling $230 million was announced. This included a Tourism Training Assistant grant scheme to help the tourism sector which was most hit by SARS. Injection of $280 million into a Skills Redevelopment Programme to help co-fund the retraining of workers and the forming of a Workforce Development Agency (WDA) to address the issues of structural unemployment due to skill mismatch.

(*Continued*)

Table 1: (*Continued*)

Event	Policy Response
2008 — Global Financial Crisis following the collapse of the sub-prime mortgage market, leading to a write-down of banks holding debt instruments tied to sub-prime mortgages. This resulted in a global withdrawal of credit from the financial system as banks stopped lending altogether due to uncertainty of the effects of the write-downs. The high interest rates and the lack of liquidity resulted in a drastic slowdown of economic activity globally.	The government provided the Resilience Package which included the following two special elements besides the usual business cost cutting measures of rebates for taxes and fees and charges: — A Jobs Credit scheme which provided businesses with cash grants based on employees' wages. This encouraged firms to keep workers employed during the downturn which was due to a liquidity issue rather than a loss of competitiveness. — Special Risk Sharing Initiative under which the government undertook 80% of the loan default risk of banks to increase the availability of credit in the supply chain. To pre-empt the withdrawals of deposits in the banking system and bank runs, the government provided a temporary guarantee on all Singapore dollar and foreign currency deposits of individual and non-bank customers in licensed banks, finance companies, and merchant banks.

acceleration of development projects to moderate the decline in the construction sector during the 1997 downturn, these were in fact projects that had been planned for implementation in the coming few years to meet social and economic needs. The record shows that the Singapore government does not initiate infrastructure projects solely for the sake of boosting the economy. This would only create white elephants requiring additional resources for maintenance down the road.

The approach taken in Singapore is markedly different from countries less dependent on trade, where governments would undertake expansionary fiscal policies to boost aggregate demand and create

Macroeconomic Impact of Budget Balances

When the Government generates a **Budget Surplus**, the Government is effectively taking out from the economy via taxes more than it is putting back into the economy as expenditures. It is a net subtraction to aggregate demand.

An increase in budget surplus constitutes a negative fiscal "impulse" that would help reduce inflationary pressures. This is appropriate when the economy is overheating (working at above the long-term potential output — the level of production at which there is no pressure for prices to rise or fall).

Conversely, a **Budget Deficit** is a net contribution to aggregate demand. An increase in the deficit or reduction in surplus equates to "pump priming" to boost the economy when it is operating at below potential.

jobs. These governments would initiate infrastructure projects, increase transfers or lower taxes so as to put more money in the hands of businesses and households who would then spend more to generate an increase in economic activity and create more jobs. But the fiscal multipliers in Singapore are simply too low for the government to pursue such expansionary fiscal policies effectively.[27]

Fiscal multipliers measure how much GDP changes for every additional dollar in government spending or reduction in taxes or revenues. Given the high savings rate in Singapore, a large percentage of the increased incomes of households and businesses would be saved rather than spent. In addition, Singapore's dependence on trade means that for every dollar spent in domestic consumption, around 40 cents would "leak" out of the economy in paying for imports.[28] Therefore, increasing government expenditures or reducing taxes to increase domestic incomes would have limited impact to boosting domestic spending.

Instead, given that the value added from exports makes up two-thirds of Singapore's GDP,[29] it would be more effective for fiscal spending to be targeted at enabling the export sector to raise productivity so that goods and services could be priced competitively to keep export levels up.

Long-Term Sustainability

Given the low fiscal multipliers in Singapore, the fiscal measures undertaken in response to recessions have generally been crafted to cushion the impact of downturns and restore economic competitiveness rather than to boost domestic demand as the main objective.

Households and businesses (especially small and medium enterprises (SMEs), which employ around two-thirds of Singapore's workforce) would receive short-term relief to help them tide through the difficult times. The government would put much care into designing the measures to achieve the greatest effect in assisting those who needed help most, for example, lower-income households. In addition, the measures are one-off so as not to breed a dependency on such transfers which would affect long-term fiscal sustainability. The assistance packages are usually termed as "special" transfers to emphasise that they are not to be expected under normal circumstances and are usually given in 1 year. If the benefits were to be extended for a few years, they would be scaled down over a few years and removed when the economy recovered.

Helping Businesses with Labour Costs to Keep Cyclical Unemployment Down

One of the key objectives of special transfers for businesses is to help keep employees on payrolls to prevent widespread unemployment. By helping workers keep their jobs, their families would also be provided for. Businesses would also preserve the capacity to respond when demand recovers. The government would also usually take the opportunity of a downturn to push through initiatives to encourage companies and workers to upgrade. For example, the government launched the Skills Programme for Upgrading and Resilience (SPUR) in the wake of the 2008 Global Financial Crisis which provided higher course fee support for companies and individuals and absentee payrolls for companies that send their workers for training. In just 6 months, 124,500 workers signed up for SPUR, including 83,500 workers sent by 1,800 companies, many of which were using SPUR to manage their excess manpower. Another 40,600 individuals signed up to upgrade their skills and 19,000 job seekers found jobs through SPUR.[30]

Prior to 2009, the government relied on CPF adjustments as the main tool to help keep workers employed during downturns by bringing wage costs down to help businesses stay competitive. However, the measure of cutting CPF contribution rates would eventually affect the sufficiency of CPF savings for retirement and healthcare needs of workers. The government would thus restore the CPF reductions as soon as economic conditions and productivity improve.

In the wake of the Global Financial Crisis in 2009, instead of cutting CPF contributions, the government undertook discretionary fiscal intervention in the form of a one-off Jobs Credit scheme to help businesses keep workers on the payroll during the downturn. This marked the first time the government helped businesses and workers using surpluses accumulated by past terms of government so that CPF rates need not be cut in a downturn. In the process, the government articulated the two principles for the use of accumulated reserves for a downturn. First, the reserves would be used only in "very exceptional situations", such as when external events or crises pose a threat to Singapore's economy or society. Second, the measures to be funded out of the reserves are to be of a temporary nature and not built into continuing government programmes.

Promoting Capability Development and Restructuring

Another consistent characteristic of the recession packages is the focus on capability development and restructuring. As a small export-oriented economy, Singapore has no choice but to ensure that it can produce goods and services at comparable if not lower costs than competing exporters in other countries. The best way to help workers and businesses over the long term is to ensure that they are productive and globally competitive.

During recessions, measures to help reduce costs for businesses, such as rebates for income taxes and fees and charges, would almost certainly be included in the fiscal packages announced by the government, but these would be temporary in nature. Cost reduction measures were undertaken to help businesses stay afloat so that the capabilities built up by businesses over the years would not be lost just because of a temporary slump. But the Singapore government does not engage in subsidising the operations of businesses simply to boost economic competitiveness and beef up employment. It would be fiscally unsustainable.

Rather, the cost reduction measures would be phased out and replaced by longer-term initiatives to encourage economic restructuring over the longer term by providing support for businesses who make investments to improve productivity and move up the value chain. For example, following the 1985 recession, the National Productivity Board (NPB) established a Management Guidance Centre in 1986 to administer various management consultancy programmes for local companies to raise productivity levels at the company level as well as industry level.[31] In the wake of the 2001 recession, the Trade and Development Board was reconstituted as International Enterprise Singapore (IE Singapore) in 2002 to help Singapore companies internationalise and develop new overseas markets. Through schemes such as Global Company Partnership and Market Readiness Assistance, IE Singapore works with Singapore-based companies in their various stages of growth towards being globally competitive. In the wake of the 2008/2009 Global Financial Crisis, the National Productivity and Continuing Education Council (NPCEC) was established in April 2010 to drive the national effort to raise the productivity at the sectoral, enterprise, and worker levels. The NPCEC taps on the National Productivity Fund, the Lifelong Learning Fund, and the Skills Development Fund to fund 10-year roadmaps developed for sectors with significant contributions to employment and GDP and which have potential for productivity gains. Over the years, these long-term initiatives have served to sustain the competitiveness of both businesses and workers by encouraging them to build on their own strengths, upgrade capabilities, and adjust strategies to meet new needs in the global economy.

Summary

As a small and open economy, Singapore is like a small ship in rough seas.

Historically, for each time its economy suffered a setback due to a global shock, Singapore rebounded quickly by making cost adjustments and restructuring its economy to ride on new drivers of global growth by building new sectors and engaging new growth markets. This is not a trivial achievement. Restructuring is often very painful for the individual participants of the economy. Workers lose their jobs and cannot find new ones without retraining. The new jobs may not pay as well as before at the beginning, and increments in wages may only be possible over time through the building up of proficiency and experience. Owners of SMEs experience anxiety as they see costs escalate at the same time as revenues fall. Many businesses had to fold up or relocate to neighbouring countries where costs were lower. But businesses that take efforts to improve productivity to reduce costs and innovate to find and serve new markets would get government support and continue contributing to Singapore's growth.

Singapore's fiscal strategies have helped enhance the resilience of the Singapore economy by providing short-term relief which prevented economic capabilities that had been built up over time from being set back if not demolished by external shocks. In addition, the government has provided support to help businesses and workers continually build on their accomplishments by upgrading themselves so that they are better prepared to weather the next downturn and enjoy income growth over the longer term. This continued ability to respond nimbly to changes in the global economy has enabled Singapore to sustain its growth as a small but open and strong economy over the last half a century despite the volatility in the global environment.

Chapter 6

Promoting Confidence through Budgetary Prudence

One of the key roles of governments is to provide macroeconomic stability, which involves maintaining stable prices to promote sustainable growth. Economists believe that there is a level at which the economy could produce without causing prices to rise or fall. This is the long-term potential output level. The economy could produce at above the potential level to meet the excessive demand for goods and services, but at higher prices. If left unchecked, a cycle of ever increasing prices could form as businesses and workers demand higher prices and wages respectively in expectation of higher inflation. A persistent increase in the general price level often discourages investment and consumption. Banks would be reluctant to lend except at high interest rates to offset the fall in the real value of debts. The resultant lower business investments eventually lead to lower long-term growth. High inflationary growth is thus unsustainable.

On the flip side, when the economy is producing below potential, employment and prices would fall. Persistent falling prices or deflation encourages people to defer spending in expectation of lower prices. The lower consumption feeds into lower investments and a

Fiscal Stabilisers

There are in built automatic stabilisers in most government budgets. Tax collections would generally increase as the economy grows and vice versa, without the government needing to do anything specifically such as changing tax rates. On the expenditure side, a large percentage is paid out as wages or payments to suppliers based on fixed rates. These are generally not very responsive to changes in GDP. Other elements of government spending, such as financial assistance payments, move in opposite direction to economic growth. For example, unemployment assistance would fall in an economic boom when unemployment rates are low and vice versa.

Taken together, when an economy grows, the budget surplus will grow (or deficit reduce) because revenues increase and expenditures fall or stay roughly the same. The resultant dampening effect on economy growth reduces inflationary pressures. The reverse holds when the economy shrinks. The reduction in surplus or deficit acts as a boost to the economy when it slows down.

The net impact of automatic stabilisers moderate the ups and downs of the economy and prevent wild swings. In severe situations, with inflation risks going out of control, additional discretionary measures such as raising of tax rates may be undertaken to supplement the effect of automatic stabilisers. Likewise, when the economy is at risk of depression, new projects may be initiated to increase spending and "pump-prime" the economy.

downward spiral of decreasing growth or increasing shrinkage of economic activities.

In most countries, governments undertake fiscal policies to contain inflation by raising taxes or lowering government expenditures. The effect would be a reduction in incomes for businesses and households, which then discourages investment and consumption spending. These are "contractionary" measures which curb "excessive" demand to bring production levels back down to potential — a "cooling" of the "overheated" economy.

On the other hand, to address deflationary risks when the economy is producing below potential, governments can reduce taxes or increase government expenditures to boost the incomes of businesses and households. These measures, which encourage higher spending on investment and consumption of goods and services, constitute "expansionary" fiscal policies that serve to lift the economy back nearer to its potential.

Given Singapore's high dependence on imports, and its inability to influence global prices as a small importer, changes in world prices or exchange rates are the major drivers of domestic inflation in Singapore. The government does not undertake "expansionary" or "contractionary" fiscal policies to manage price levels but depends on the conduct of monetary policy by the Monetary Authority of Singapore (MAS) to maintain price stability. The MAS manages the "imported" inflation by pegging the Singapore dollar exchange rates within a band against a weighted basket of currencies of Singapore's major trading partners. When the Singapore exchange rate strengthens, prices of imports to Singaporeans are brought down. The exchange rate also affects the prices of services and goods produced by Singapore relative to its competitors, thereby influencing the level of aggregate demand for exports. For example, when the Singapore dollar appreciates, the prices of its exports become more expensive in terms of foreign currencies. Lower demand for the pricier exports translates to lower production and employment. Unlike the central banks in some countries, the MAS does not manage the money supply or interest rates to manage aggregate demand because of Singapore's openness to capital flows as a financial center. It would be very difficult for MAS to intervene in the capital market to influence interest rates, as differences between domestic and foreign interest rates would be arbitrated away quickly by large and quick capital flows.

Therefore, interest and inflation rates in Singapore are determined most directly by international interest rates and expected movements of the Singapore exchange rates, which are managed by MAS to prevent excessive short-term fluctuations. Over the medium term, MAS ensures that the exchange rate moves with local and global economic fundamentals and market conditions to keep inflation low for sustained economic growth. This has provided the macroeconomic stability which is conducive for trade and investment activities.

Fiscal Sustainability: Key to Stable Currency to Promote Investment and Trade

Fiscal sustainability is nonetheless an important part of Singapore's macroeconomic stability. The effective implementation of MAS's monetary policies to influence inflation is fundamentally premised on sustainable fiscal policies. First, all Singapore dollar notes and coins issued by the MAS are required by law to be backed fully by assets, which means that the government cannot print money to finance budget deficits if it does not have the assets to back up the additional money issued. Second, the MAS maintains official foreign reserves (OFRs) to intervene in the foreign exchange markets for its day-to-day operations to keep the Singapore dollar within the trade weighted band. A prudent fiscal policy, which contributes to the maintenance of budget surpluses, is necessary for MAS's operations.

The government started accumulating its budgetary reserves in the 1970s. Budget surpluses had grown along with the GDP, which grew four-fold from 1966 to 1980 (at 1985 prices) with an annual average of 10.3%.[32] The policy to accumulate budgeted surpluses has provided a substantial war chest for the MAS to undertake its monetary policies to keep the Singapore dollar stable against the currencies of major trading partners. In fact, the MAS maintains an OFR that is more than what most central banks need for day-to-day monetary operations. In addition, the government stands ready to inject more of its reserves into MAS when needed. This serves as a deterrence against currency attacks on the Singapore dollar. When that happens, MAS would have the resources on hand to ensure that potential speculators who try to sell down the Singapore dollar would end up suffering a loss.

A stable Singapore dollar encourages trading activities by reducing the uncertainty of trade prices. The long-term commitment to a stable Singapore dollar backed by sizeable reserves and maintained by sustainable fiscal policies also gives confidence to foreign investors that their capital investments in Singapore would pay off over the expected useful lives of the assets, and the value of their investments would be safeguarded. This provided the policy predictability that MNCs needed for their long-range planning. Foreign direct investment (FDI) has thus continued to flow into Singapore, boosting productivity and enabling the local industrial sector to move up the value chain over the years.

Creating Reserves for a Rainy Day

The budgetary reserves also serve as a critical resource to secure Singapore's future. As a strategic asset, the reserves provide a key defence for Singapore by buffering the country from crises and enabling Singapore to mount a speedy response. Any budget deficit arising from additional discretionary spending during a crisis could be financed by the surpluses accumulated from previous growth years. Singapore's strong reserves position has provided assurance to the public and investors that the government has the resources to intervene strongly and decisively to provide a soft landing in a crisis.

The Singapore economy is heavily dependent on exports. As around two-thirds of the goods and services produced in Singapore are exported, employment is also highly dependent on export growth. The availability of past reserves gives investors the confidence that Singapore has the ability to help businesses restore cost competitiveness to boost exports and keep employment up through fiscal measures rather than through the indirect means of changes in the exchange rate. MAS is thus allowed to focus on its objective of maintaining price stability and a strong and stable Singapore dollar regardless of the volatility in Singapore's economic growth rates.

Generating Returns to Keep Taxes Low

The budget surpluses accumulated by the government are also invested to earn dividend and interest incomes. Up to half of the total investment returns, which includes the dividend and interest yields as well as the capital appreciation, is taken into the annual budget to finance government expenditures, while the remainder of the returns are reinvested. Therefore, the value of the accumulated surpluses appreciates in real terms over the longer term and continues to grow in tandem with economic growth, even as the stream of income generated by the accumulated surpluses helps fund the growing needs of the population.

In fact, the source of investment income has enabled the government to cut taxes from 2001 to enhance Singapore's attractiveness to investors as lower-cost regional competitors for FDI emerged. Government operating revenues had thus fallen from over 20% of GDP in the mid-1990s to around 17% of GDP today.[33] While public expenditure has largely kept pace with economic growth, and remained low at between 12% and 18% of GDP from 1999 to 2016, the government was able to sustain the low taxes without incurring debts by drawing on the investment returns on the accumulated surpluses for its annual budgetary spending. The low taxes served to increase the after-tax profitability of businesses and the take-home pay of workers. At the same time, the supply and quality of public services continued to improve over the years through public sector innovation and reliance on market competition in the delivery of public services.

Summary

Together with MAS's monetary operations, the fiscal policy of generating a modest budget surplus over the medium term has contributed to a strong and stable Singapore dollar that supported low inflationary growth since Singapore's independence. It has also provided a fiscal buffer that allows the government to respond flexibly via discretionary measures in a cyclical downturn while keeping taxes low to enhance Singapore's competitiveness. Overall, Singapore's prudent fiscal policy has contributed to macroeconomic stability over the years which gave businesses the confidence to continue investing in Singapore for sustained economic growth.

Chapter 7

Protection of Accumulated Surpluses

Singapore's accumulated fiscal surpluses were first placed in MAS to be managed by MAS as foreign reserves. These were invested mainly in short-term assets to meet the monetary operational needs that MAS has to fulfil in order to manage the Singapore exchange rate. However, the fund size soon grew beyond what MAS needed for its operational needs, and it did not make sense to invest all the funds in short-term assets that yielded low returns. In 1981, the Government Investment Corporation (GIC) was formed to manage the "long-term" foreign reserves more strategically and professionally to earn higher returns. This allowed MAS to concentrate on its central banking functions. The mandate given to GIC was to preserve the international purchasing power of the "non-monetary" component of Singapore's financial reserves and earn a rate of return to enhance the value of the national savings.

Establishment of Professional Agencies to Manage Singapore's Reserves

The GIC was created as a separate entity from the government to ensure that the reserves would be managed professionally by the best talent recruited from the open market, both in Singapore and abroad. Its separation from the government also allows GIC to embark on long-term investment strategies and take calculated risks, such as investing in new and emerging markets (or new asset classes) as needed to attain good returns, without undue bureaucratic or political interference. Over the years, the funds managed by GIC has grown from several billion Singapore dollars in 1981 to "well over a hundred billion US dollars (USD)" now. The GIC has achieved returns on the funds at rates comparable to high-return asset classes of equities in nominal USD terms since 1981 with less risk.[34]

The Singapore government also had substantial ownership in commercial and industrial undertakings such as airlines, telecommunications, and banks. When the Singapore government was developing the industrial sector in the 1960s, it had provided loans through EDB to some companies, and co-invested in others, in order to encourage investors to create jobs in Singapore. In 1968, the various industrial loans were consolidated and put together under the Development Bank of Singapore, which was later corporatised to form DBS Bank. When the British Armed Forces withdrew in 1971, the government converted the British naval yards to ship repair yards, and naval workshops became engineering companies. By 1974, the Singapore government owned 35 companies and miscellaneous investments, including the Singapore Airlines which was set up to develop international routes out of Singapore to enhance its air connectivity. Temasek Holdings (Temasek) was set up to take over the equity ownership so that these companies would be run as separate commercial entities from the government which was conflicted as the policy maker and regulator.[35] Although the shares of Temasek are owned by the Singapore Minister for Finance,[g] the companies held by Temasek operate on equal terms with other private sector firms and do not receive any additional operational grants or subsidies from the government.

---

[g] Under the Singapore Minister for Finance (Incorporation) Act (Chapter 183), the Minister for Finance is a body corporate that holds moveable and immovable properties on behalf of the state.

They are subject to competitive pressures to operate efficiently and expected to make profits and yield dividends to Temasek. If the companies do not come up to expectations, they would be divested. Like GIC, Temasek recruits its own staff from the market and their management and operational decisions are undertaken as a commercial entity separate from the government. Over the years, as its portfolio companies grew in size and profitability in tandem with the growth of the economy, Temasek evolved from just an investment holding company to become an equity investor. Subsequently, Temasek shifted its strategy from one focused mainly on Singapore to also invest in profitable companies overseas. This enabled Temasek to grow its portfolio to a significant size. As at 31 March 2016, Temasek's portfolio was $242 billion (US$180 billion) and Temasek's compounded annualised total shareholder return since inception in 1974 was 15% in Singapore dollar terms or 17% in US dollar terms.[36]

In summary, Singapore's financial reserves are managed by three agencies — MAS, GIC, and Temasek. MAS manages the investments of the reserves mainly for its monetary operations. Most of its assets are in lower-risk, shorter-term assets. Besides the non-monetary component of the reserves, GIC also manages the assets backing the government's liabilities, such as the government securities issued to the CPF and on the market, which are all guaranteed. Unlike GIC which invests in a diversified portfolio across asset classes, including bonds and equities, and across geographies, Temasek is an active, equities-only investor, taking higher risks to achieve higher returns over time.[37]

Constitutional Framework to Govern Spending of Reserves

The policy of generating a modest budget surplus over the economic cycle has over the years resulted in the accumulation of substantial "past reserves" — the term that Singapore government uses for the budget surpluses accumulated by previous terms of government. Given the size of the past reserves and its importance to sustaining

---

Triggering Presidential Approval for the Use of Past Reserves

The requirement for presidential approval to tap on the past reserves was tested in the wake of the 2008 Global Financial Crisis. In October 2008, the President approved a $150 billion guarantee on all bank deposits in Singapore to be backed by past reserves. Though Singapore's banking and financial system was stable and not at risk, the guarantee was needed to prevent a capital outflow following the introduction of bank guarantees elsewhere in the region. This guarantee expired on 31 Dec 2010 without being triggered.

For the budget that followed in January 2009, the government obtained the president's approval to draw down $4.9 billion from the past reserves to fund special schemes (Jobs Credit Scheme and the Special Risk-Sharing Initiative). The economy rebounded strongly to grow by 14.5% in 2010. The amount actually drawn was lower than budgeted at $4.0 billion. In February 2011, the government decided to return the amount to past reserves in view that it had accumulated sufficient surpluses over its term.

Singapore's growth strategy, the Singapore government amended the constitution in 1991 to ensure good governance and management of the reserves. This served to address political concerns that the past reserves would be squandered away by a populist government. The constitutional amendments in 1991 enshrined the following fiscal requirements under what has been termed the "Past Reserves Protection" framework.

Ensuring Balanced Budgets

Under the Past Reserves Protection framework, the government is required to balance its budgets over its term. Each new term of government must generate its own revenues to finance its own plans. Any deficit must be financed by surpluses generated in the earlier years during its term. Surpluses accumulated by every government would be "locked up" at the end of its term, that is, it would not be available for spending by the next term of government unless with the approval of both the parliament and the President. Every budget must first be approved by parliament before it is sent to the President for his final endorsement. The President, who is elected through a national vote, would have the mandate to veto the government's budget even after its approval by the parliament if he is of the view that any deficits would lead to the government drawing on past reserves to finance any expenditure.[h]

Restrictions on Borrowing

The government is not able to borrow without the approvals of the President and the parliament. The premise is that borrowings are in fact liabilities that run down past reserves in the future. An exception is provided to this rule however, for issuance of Singapore Government Securities (SGS) to develop the Singapore bond market and to provide a return to CPF (which invests in Special SGS to earn a return for CPF members). The proceeds from these borrowings are governed by legislation, which require the funds to be fully invested into assets which earn a return. The interest and principal payments on the SGS are made out from the investments.

Protection of Key State Assets

Besides financial assets, land assets are also classified as past reserves. Under the Past Reserves Protection framework, key state assets — land and financial assets — are deemed to be past reserves. These cannot be liquidated for spending, that is, they are "locked up". Proceeds from the sale of land or divestment of financial assets cannot be spent in the annual budget. Any transactions involving the

---

[h] Under the constitution, the President has to seek the advice of a Council of Presidential Advisers before he vetoes the government budget. If the president vetoes the budget against the advice of the council, the parliament can overturn the president's veto with a two-thirds majority.

sale of land and financial assets owned by the state can only be undertaken at fair market value (FMV). If any transactions are undertaken below FMV, the shortfall must be paid out of the government budget (and be locked away as past reserves, the spending out of which must have the approvals of both the elected President and parliament).

Application to Statutory Boards

The Past Reserves Protection framework is applicable to the government, but it is also applied to Temasek, GIC, MAS, and CPF,[i] which manage substantial financial assets, as well as to government agencies responsible for significant land assets such as the JTC and the HDB.

Net Investment Returns Contributions to the Budget

Until 2001, investment incomes — the interest and dividend incomes from the reserves — had been taken into the budget for spending without any requirement to reinvest the investment income. There was no clear policy on how the incomes generated from the reserves were to be used effectively.

Net Investment Income Framework Implemented in 2001

In 2001, the constitution was amended to introduce the Net Investment Income (NII) framework to lock up at least 50% of the NII earned from past reserves. Under the NII framework, the government can only spend up to 50% of the dividend and interest

---

[i]The assets under the CPF do not belong to the government, i.e., the funds are the savings of CPF account holders. However, the government decided to include CPF in the framework so that the people's CPF savings can also benefit from the protection mechanisms under the framework.

incomes received by the state, after deducting debt servicing and investment-related costs. This change underlined the government's commitment to continue growing the past reserves for future generations, even if part of the investment income is spent on current needs.

However, as actual dividend and interest incomes were dependent on market conditions, it was very difficult for the government to make NII forecasts for budgetary needs. In addition, the NII only addressed how the actual dividend and interest incomes received were to be used. It did not reflect the reality that investment returns also include significant capital gains.

Net Investment Returns Contributions Framework Implemented in 2008

In 2008, the constitution was amended to provide for Net Investment Returns (NIR) Contributions to the annual budget. Under the NIR framework, the government can spend up to 50% of the "Expected Long Term Real Rates of Return" on the past reserves. The elements of the "Expected Long Term Real Rates of Return" framework are elaborated as follows:

(i) The investment returns to be made available for spending should be based not only on income and dividends but also on capital gains and losses;

(ii) The rate of returns to be applied on the assets to determine the amount that could be used for spending in the annual budget is net of inflation in line with preserving the purchasing power of Singapore's past reserves; and

(iii) The expectation of long-term returns is based on the underlying fundamentals driving the returns of the assets over the long-term horizon which is not affected by short-term market movements due to sentiments and seasonal factors. Compared to actual dividend and capital returns, the concept removes the volatility of the NII taken into the budget for spending. In addition, the returns will be applied on the average values of the assets over a number of years so that large variations in values due to market cycles could be smoothed out.

The NIR framework came into force in budget 2009, and it enabled the government to spend $7.0 billion from the reserves as opposed to $4.3 billion the previous year.[38] From 2009 to 2014, the NIR framework was applied only on the financial reserves managed by GIC and MAS. The reserves managed by Temasek were not included given that its investment strategy was still evolving, having just begun on a shift in its strategy to invest in more geographies and sectors since 2002. Furthermore, there were no established methodologies for projecting the long-term expected real return for Temasek's portfolio, which was built up from concentrated stakes and making direct investments.

In 2015, the government amended the constitution to include the assets managed by Temasek into the NIR framework after Temasek had largely completed the implementation of its new investment strategies. By then, the government also had several years' experience of operating the NIR framework and was more confident that it could apply the framework on the assets managed by Temasek. Temasek's portfolio was consequently included into the NIR framework from 2016. The inclusion of Temasek's portfolio into the NIR bolstered Singapore's fiscal resources significantly by allowing the government to draw on the past reserves in the form of Net Investment Returns (NIR) Contribution of $14.4 billion in 2016 (revised budget) and $14.11 billion in 2017 (budgeted), compared with $9.9 billion in 2015 (revised).[39]

Summary

By generating a return that could be spent by the government in the annual budget, the past reserves provides a tremendous advantage for Singapore which enables it to keep taxes low while making critical investments to build up its economic capabilities. The Protection of

Past Reserves framework also provides a safeguard that enables the reserves to continue growing in tandem with the economy to provide sizeable OFRs to support a stable Singapore dollar, and a strong balance sheet that buffers Singapore in times of crisis.

Chapter 8

Conservatism in Fiscal Planning

At the parliamentary debate in 2008 to amend the constitution, the then Finance Minister Tharman Shanmugaratnam said that the NIR framework "would allow us to take in more for spending but not so much as to prevent our reserves from growing in line with the economy and providing for future generations." Indeed, by removing the budgetary uncertainties arising from the NII framework, the NIR framework now provides a stable stream of income for the Singapore government to commit to long-term programmes and investments without having to raise taxes. Further, the inclusion of expected capital gains over the long term have allowed the government to draw more from the reserves for current spending.

Conservative Provisions in the NIR Framework

Nevertheless, the following layers of conservatism had been introduced into the NIR framework as safeguards against overspending of the reserves.

First, the application of real returns, which is net of inflation and lower than actual returns, means that the government can draw from the reserves for spending only after ensuring that the reserves have grown by at least the inflation rate to preserve the purchasing power of the reserves.

Second, only half of the returns after setting aside for inflation rate could be spent. This means that the other half would be put back into reserves and could be reinvested to keep the reserves growing in real terms. Over the 20-year period that ended 31 March 2016, the GIC portfolio generated an annualised real return of 4.0% above global infla-tion.[40] Assuming that the expected long-term real rates of return on reserves are also at around 4%, the government would spend half of the returns (2%) and add the remainder 2% back to the reserves. At 2%, the growth of reserves would keep pace with economic growth which is expected to be in the 2%–3% range in the future.[41]

Third, the expected long-term real returns framework is to be applied on the reserves after deducting the liabilities of the govern-ment, namely in issued government securities. This means that the securities issued by the government would be backed by financial assets in terms of not only the principal amount but also the full returns on the assets managed by MAS and GIC, which typically exceed the interest to be paid on the liabilities.

As a matter of governance, the expected long-term rates of returns were to be proposed by the respective agencies managing the reserves. These were to be certified by the Minister for Finance, before being submitted to the President for approval each year. If the President, after consulting the Council of Presidential Advisers, is of the view that any of the proposed expected long-term rates of return were not rea-sonable, he could withhold his approval for the relevant rate of return to be applied to the underlying assets to derive the NIR Contribution to the annual budget. If an agreement cannot be reached, the fall back would be to adopt the long-term historical real rate returns achieved on the financial assets. This process safeguards against the possibility of the government deriving an unsustainable NIR Contribution to the budget for spending.

Extra-Budgetary Cash Flows

The application of the NIR framework may impede the ability of the agencies managing the reserves, that is, GIC, MAS and Temasek, to achieve optimisation of the returns on the reserves that they manage if the expectation to generate a certain level of cash for spending by the government lead the agencies to liquidate the financial assets managed by the agencies. This concern is mitigated by the significant extra-budgetary cash flows that are being generated by the government, which it could draw from to fund the NIR Contributions to the annual budget without encroaching on the investment cash flows of the agencies to operationalise the NIR framework.

The budget statement presented by the Singapore government excludes as revenues Capital Receipts, which comprise largely Land Sales Revenue, and Investment and Interest Income (which are receipts from financial assets held by the government). These incomes earned from past reserves, i.e. state-owned land and financial assets, are not available for spending by the government under the Reserves Protection framework.

Besides the annual operating revenues that the government raises to fund its annual expenditures, government's land sales has generated between $8.2 billion (estimated sales of land in FY2017) and $18.3 billion in cash inflows from 2012 to 2017. These are offset by Land-Related Expenditures (the bulk of which are attributed to land reclamation and land acquisition costs) which have been significantly lower than the revenues from land sales, due to the physical limits on the scale of reclamation or acquisition that can be done in any one year. In 2017, land sales revenue was estimated to be $8.2 billion while Land-Related Expenditure was budgeted at $3.0 billion.

Investment and Interest Income is another source of cash inflow that has generated between $7.1 billion and $10.5 billion (FY2017 estimated) over the same period.[42] Although the government has as a matter of practice, transferred budget surpluses into endowment or trust funds for funding of specific needs, such fund transfers are in fact book entries that do not result in actual cash outflows from the government until the funds are drawn down later. In addition, only the interest income on endowment funds could be used. The size of trust funds is much smaller in scale compared to Investment and Interest Income. Therefore, inflows from Investment and Interest Income have far exceeded the outflows from endowment and trust funds. In

2016, the total amounts drawn down from endowment and trust funds added to $4.5 billion,[43] well below the $9.6 billion in Investment and Interest Income in estimated receipts within the same year.

Since the Land-Related Expenditures can be matched against Land Sales Revenue, and Expenditures from Endowment and Trust Funds netted off Investment and Interest Income and Transfers to Endowment and Trust Funds, the net cash flow impact of the annual budget can be simply restated as follows:

Cash Surplus/Deficit ≈
Budget Balance as Presented by the Singapore Government

Add: Net realisation of land values (Land Sales less Land-Related Expenditures)
Add: Net financial fund flows (Interest and Investment Income + Transfers to Endowment and Trust Funds – Expenditures from Endowment and Trust Funds).

As shown in Fig. 2, the Singapore government has in fact enjoyed significant cash surpluses since 1990, after taking into account all the cash flows described above.

The cash surpluses have trended down from 2000 onwards after the government embarked on its tax reforms to bring income taxes down and implemented the NIR framework from 2009 to draw more from the past reserves into the budget for spending. The contributors to the positive surpluses since then have been mainly land sales revenues and actual investment and interest incomes received from the investments and loans held by the government. This reached the lowest level in 2009 at 1.6% of GDP in the aftermath of the Global Financial Crisis, when the fall in tax revenues due to the recession was accompanied by a decline in land sales revenue and investment income because of the contagion effect of the Global Financial Crisis on the property and financial markets. Nevertheless, the surplus position recovered to between 4.4% and 9.2% of GDP in the following years until 2015.

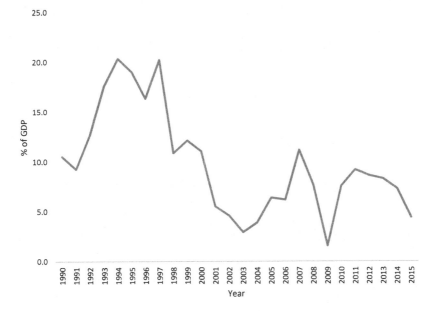

Figure 2: General Government Cash Surplus (% of GDP).

Source: 1990–2012: IMF Government Finance Statistics; 2013–2015: constructed by the author from the *Year Book of Statistics Singapore, 2016.*

Maintenance of Cash Balances

Even if cash flows were to fall to negative in any 1 year due to the vagaries of the economy, the government would have had a substantial cash balance, totalling $127 billion as at 31 March 2016,[44] which it can tap on to fund the NIR Contribution to the budget. In addition, the government can also tap on the accumulated surpluses of statutory boards (but not the surpluses of JTC, HDB, MAS, and CPF which are protected as past reserves) by calling for the statutory boards to remit the accumulated reserves to the government. For example, the Maritime Port Authority, which accumulated surpluses totalling $1.25 billion and a cash account of $682 million as at

31 December 2015,[45] can afford to return several hundred million dollars in cash to the government when called upon to do so.

Taken together, at the current levels of operating revenues and expenditures, the government has more than enough cash flow buffers to ensure that the NIR framework in its current form would not require the investment agencies to liquidate its investments to provide the cash flows to supplement the annual budget under the NIR framework. However, as the buffer in cash surpluses narrows, the government would need to pay attention to the impact on government cash flows if it were to amend the NIR framework further or if its investment agencies engage in investment strategies that result in higher Expected Long Term Real Rates of Return that would result in higher NIR Contributions drawn down for spending in the budget.

Chapter 9
Funding of Future Liabilities

Central Provident Fund

Another key pillar of fiscal strategies in Singapore is the creation of the Central Provident Fund (CPF) scheme, which reduces the government's liabilities to provide for the retirement needs for the workforce.

Many countries operate public pension schemes to support a minimum standard of living for workers who have retired. These have traditionally been in the form of cash payouts after a certain specified age, which would continue for the rest of the retiree's life. Such pension schemes work well when the population is young and growing such that contributions to the pension funds by the working population exceed withdrawals from the funds by retirees. But inadvertently with life expectancy increases, the reduced contributions of a shrinking workforce to the pension funds can no longer sustain the withdrawals by an increasing pool of retirees. Adjustments to the withdrawal age, reduction in payout amounts, and increases to pension contributions must then be effected for the pension system to remain self-sustained. Unfortunately, these are painful and unpopular changes, and governments often defer making them, choosing instead to absorb the ballooning pension expenditures and incur fiscal deficits, which are paid for by ever-increasing debts. Such unsustainable public pension schemes contribute to a set of liabilities which future governments would eventually have to pay off by making even more painful adjustments such as tax increases, expenditure cuts, or state asset sales. The worst-case outcome would be the printing of money to fund the liabilities, which would only lead to high inflation, decrease in the value of savings, and loss of investor confidence in the economy. Unsustainable pension systems are in effect benefits paid for by future generations.

Singapore does not have a public pension scheme. Instead, the CPF provides for the retirement needs of workers. The compulsory CPF savings scheme requires all employers and employees to contribute a portion of the employee's monthly gross salary to the employee's savings account maintained by the CPF board. The size of the account at the end of the employee's working life would determine the level of payouts that the employee would be entitled to when he retires. Over the years, the Singapore government has made changes to the CPF system to allow CPF accounts to be used for specific purposes such as education and healthcare as CPF balances grew.

Currently, the CPF contributions from the employee and his or her employer are segregated into the MediSave, Special, and Ordinary accounts. A certain share of the CPF contributions (8% of wage for employees below age 35, progressively increased for older workers to 10.5% of wage for employees above age 50) is allocated first to the employee's MediSave account, which can only be used for specific medical care and hospitalisation expenses and to purchase medical insurance. This is followed by between 1% and 11.5% of the employee's wage, depending on the employee's age, to be allocated to the Special account, which the employee can use for investments into approved financial assets if he wishes to earn a higher return than the interest rate provided by the CPF board. The remainder is then allocated to the Ordinary account which can be used for housing, education as well as investment. The Special and MediSave accounts earn higher interest rates as the amounts are expected to be kept for longer terms as the Special Account could only be drawn down on retirement and the Medisave Account for hospitalisation and specific medical expenses. To ensure that the retiree will receive payouts from the CPF savings over his lifetime, the CPF Life scheme was implemented in 2010 to provide

CPF Contribution Rates as percentage of employee's pay	
Employees aged 55 and below: 20%	Employers: 17%

Distributed to sub-accounts

	Ordinary Account	Special Account	MediSave
Allowable uses	Home ownership Education Investment	Investment	Healthcare
Interest rates:	Derived from local short-term rates, with a floor of 2.5%	Derived from an average 10-year Singapore government security yield + 1% (floor of 4%)	Derived from an average 10-year Singapore government security yield + 1% (floor of 4%)

The first $60,000 of CPF balances earns an extra 1% for all CPF members. An additional 1% extra interest on the first $30,000 of CPF balances will be provided for members aged 55 and above.

Ordinary and Special accounts merged into Retirement account at age 55.

An amount above the "Retirement Sums"[k] could be withdrawn at 55. The Retirement Sum is required to be invested into CPF Life for monthly payouts over the employee's lifetime after retirement.	MediSave Minimum Sum to be set aside for Healthcare needs

Figure 3: Schematic Representation of the CPF Scheme.

a monthly payout for the employee after retirement.[j] The payout amount under the CPF Life scheme would be based on the savings of the employee when he or she reaches age 55. The CPF scheme that has been effective from 1 Jan 2016 is summarised in Fig. 3.

The CPF scheme has enabled the Singapore government to ensure that liabilities to future retirees in terms of expected retirement and health benefits are reflected in the CPF's balance sheets and fully backed by the employees' savings. The CPF board invests the savings into Special Singapore Government Security (SSGS) bonds that pay

[j] CPF Life pools together the savings of all CPF retirees to pay the retirees a monthly sum over the lifetimes of the retirees.

[k] Determined by the government, the Retirement Sum amounts are regularly reviewed and adjusted to ensure that CPF members enjoy a regular income from the payout eligibility age to support a basic standard of living.

Singapore's Sovereign Debt Fully Backed by Assets

Some international reports such as the CIA Public Debt Factbook and the World Economic Forum report have reflected Singapore as having a public debt exceeding 100% of GDP, at levels close to Greece before its sovereign debt crisis in 2010.

Singapore's high debt levels are not a cause for concern however. The public debt incurred by Singapore arises from the Singapore government securities (SGSs) and special Singapore government securities (SSGS) issued by the Singapore government.

SGSs are issued to develop the domestic debt market. They provide a risk-free benchmark against which other risky market instruments are priced off.

SSGS are non-tradable bonds issued specifically to meet the investment needs of the CPF. Singaporeans' CPF monies are invested in these special securities which are fully guaranteed by the government. The securities earn for the CPF board a coupon rate that is pegged to CPF interest rates that members receive.

All the borrowing proceeds are invested and thus backed by financial assets, which yield a return more than sufficient to cover the debt servicing costs.

The Singapore government has accumulated substantial surpluses over many years and has assets well in excess of its liabilities. Singapore is in fact a net creditor country.

---

interest rates to ensure that the real value of the savings are maintained. As CPF savings belong to employees, employees are incentivised to stay employed in order to build up their assets. The Ordinary account gives employees the opportunity to build up their physical (home ownership) and virtual (education) assets, while the Special and MediSave accounts provide them with the safety nets for retirement and healthcare needs.

As long as the majority of Singaporeans stay employed and have sufficient balances in their CPF accounts, the Singapore government could charge Singaporeans a fair share of the costs of public housing, education, and medical services which could be paid out of CPF savings. Singaporeans would also economise on the amounts spent on these needs and not overconsume in these areas because they are required to pay for the consumption from their CPF savings.

CPF has thus enabled the Singapore government to reduce public spending in the areas of housing, education, and medical services. It is a key plank of the Singapore government's fiscal policy to keep public expenditures lower than many developed countries while ensuring fiscal sustainability and delivering the same or better outcomes. It also ensures intergenerational equity by ensuring that the benefits enjoyed by each generation of retirees are not left to be paid for by future generations.

Government Securities Fund

Besides the CPF scheme, the Singapore government has also set up various other funds to ensure that foreseeable future government liabilities are provided for sufficiently. In particular, the Singapore government maintains a significant Government Securities Fund (GSF) amounting to $461 billion as at 31 March 2016.[46] The government issues Singapore Government Securities to develop the domestic bond market and the proceeds of the issues are placed in the GSF, which are invested to yield a return that goes back into the Fund. The interest expense and redemption of the Singapore government securities are paid out of the GSF. The GSF therefore ensures that the liabilities arising from the issuance of the government securities are more than fully provided for.

Government Trust Funds

Under the Reserves Protection framework, the Singapore government can "pledge" its current reserves (budget surpluses accumulated during the current term of government, which are not locked up as past reserves under the framework) into trust funds for the financing of any special projects initiated during the current term of government. For example, in announcing the special "Pioneer Package" initiative, which would provide additional healthcare subsidies to the first-generation Singaporeans born on or before 31 December 1949, the government created the Pioneer Generation Fund into which $8 billion was injected from the government's current reserves for the expected expenditures under the Pioneer Generation Package. Other examples include the GST Tax Voucher fund, set up in 2012 to fund the permanent GST Tax Voucher scheme to help offset the goods and services tax (GST) paid by lower-income households and the Special Employment Credit Fund to offset the part of the employer CPF contribution rates for older workers. These trust funds are set aside by the Singapore government to finance the tail of spending commitments arising from special initiatives announced within each term of government. Similar trust funds are also set up to ensure the continuity of spending in certain priorities, such as improving national productivity and investing in R&D. The National Productivity Fund and the National Research Fund were set up to assure investors of Singapore's commitment to continue upgrading its economy regardless of the vagaries of economic cycles. The government has committed to top up these trust funds as and when the budget allows. In FY2016, spending from the various trust funds is estimated to add up to about $3.7 billion.[47]

Endowment Funds

In addition to trust funds, the Singapore government also regularly makes transfers from its annual budgets into endowment funds, whenever it has the budget surpluses to do so. Endowment funds have been set up to meet specific needs in education, healthcare, and community care since the 1990s. While the principal amounts of these endowment funds cannot be spent, they generate a stream of interest incomes, which represent Singapore's commitment to ensure a minimum level of spending for the purposes represented by each endowment fund. As at 31 March 2016, the amounts of funds set aside as endowment funds for specific purposes total more than $20 billion[35] (details in Table 2).

These funds earn an interest rate of up to 4% annually,[1] which serve as extra-budgetary resources that complement the annual

---

[1] Pegged to the interest rate paid on savings in CPF Special accounts.

Table 2: Details of Endowment Funds Set Up by the Singapore Government.

Endowment Funds	Amount (in millions of Dollars)	Purposes
EduSave	6,469	To fund scholarships, awards, and bursaries in schools as well as enrichment activities for students.
LifeLong Learning	4,962	To fund continuous education and training of the workforce.
Medical	4,120	Also known as MediFund, it is used to offset medical expenses of the lower-income households.
ElderCare	2,882	To offset expenses in lower-income households in eldercare.
Community Care (Comcare)	1,713	To fund programmes to address social needs in the community.
Total	20,146	

budget to provide additional fiscal support for low-income families in the area of healthcare, education, and other social needs. Spending from the government's endowment funds was estimated at $724 million in FY 2016.

Summary

The practice of setting aside funds to meet future foreseeable liabilities and provide for future needs of the nation has served to reduce the future fiscal burdens on the nation. By ensuring that all liabilities are backed by assets, the Singapore government maintains the fiscal space for it to respond to shocks and unanticipated needs in a sustainable way. It also ensures intergenerational equity by not leaving liabilities to be paid for by future generations.

Chapter 10

Capping Expenditures, Creating Value

Revenue Structure

As shown in Fig. 4, the Singapore government raises its revenues through a variety of channels such as taxes, fees, and other charges. Indirect taxes make up more than half of total operating revenues (before taking into account income from investments). Nevertheless, corporate income tax (CIT) and personal income tax (PIT) are among the top three taxes collected, with GST in the second place in terms of yields. The fiscal sustainability of the Singapore government depends critically on these three highest taxes.[48] Together, CIT, PIT, and GST make up more than half of total operating revenues.

Revenue Buoyancy

There is a "buoyancy" in government revenues, that is, the revenues grow as the economy grows even as tax rates are not increased. Buoyancy measures the change in revenue for a given change in GDP. A buoyancy of "1" means that revenue grows by 1% for every 1% growth in GDP. Based on a study[49] undertaken by the Ministry of

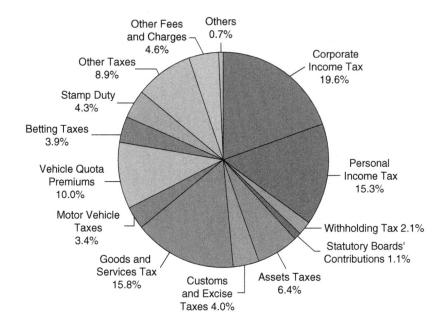

Figure 4: Contributions of Taxes, Fees, and Charges to Government Operating Revenues (FY2016).

Finance (MOF) in 2006, PIT has a higher buoyancy than CIT (1.2 compared to 1.0), reflecting the progressive nature of PIT as opposed to CIT which is a flat tax. The estimated buoyancy for GST over the period FY1985–FY2004 was estimated to be 1.5, but this figure reflected an increase in GST rate from 3% to 4% in 2003 and to 5% in 2004.[m] The underlying buoyancy (assuming no change in rates) would probably be lower if the effects of the rate increase are taken into account. Among the indirect taxes, motor vehicle taxes and customs and excise taxes (on tobacco, liquor, and petroleum products) appear to be the least buoyant. The share of motor vehicle taxes in total operating revenue has fallen from 5% in FY2004 to 2.8% in 2015. Customs and excise taxes have shrunk 7% in FY2004 to 5% over the same period. Table 3 reproduces the buoyancies computed by MOF in the 2006 study.

---

[m] GST was further increased to the current 7% in 2007.

Table 3:   Tax Buoyancies by Tax Types.

Tax Types	FY1985–2000	1985–2004
CIT	1.1	1.0
PIT	1.2	1.2
GST	0.9	1.5
Customs and excise taxes	0.4	0.4
Motor vehicle taxes	0.8	0.6

According to the MOF study, the buoyancy of Singapore's operating revenues taken together is around 1, i.e., the revenues grow 1% for every 1% growth in GDP. In another the study in 2009,[50] MOF computed the correlation of all revenues to GDP over 1998–2007 as 0.92. One can safely conclude that government operating revenues change at roughly the rate at which GDP changes at the aggregate level.

Block Budget

The buoyancy of revenues meant that the Singapore government can spend more without incurring deficits as long as the expenditures do not grow faster than the economy. This is the basis for the block budget system adopted by the MOF. Under this system, the budget for every ministry is capped at an agreed level based on historical spending trends and projected needs. To ensure that expenditures do not inadvertently outgrow revenues over the medium term, budget caps are provided a "growth factor" set at a percentage of smoothened GDP (sGDP), which is an "average" measure of GDP based on the growth rates of the past 3 years' GDP, current year GDP, and 3 years' GDP projected forward. Since the buoyancy of operating revenues is around 1, operating revenues would more than keep pace with expenditure growth to ensure that the budget increases are sustainable.

The pegging of expenditures to sGDP also provides an automatic stabiliser in the fiscal system. Based on this formula, yearly expenditures will grow less than revenues when the economy is growing, thereby contributing to a growing surplus. When the economy is shrinking, expenditures will also reduce at a slower rate than revenues, leading to larger deficits. Over the medium term, the block budget system moderates fluctuations in aggregate demand, although as discussed earlier in Chapter 5, the impact is muted because of the small fiscal multiplier in Singapore. More importantly, compared to the GDP of a single year, the smoothing effect provided by the sGDP formula reduces the volatility of government spending (since Singapore's GDP is rather volatile), thereby providing certainty for expenditure planning by the ministries involved.

In addition to ensuring that the Singapore government spends within its means and providing stability, the block budget system provides for flexibility and responsiveness in budgets. Ministries are given the budgets in "blocks" over the medium term and do not need to negotiate the budgets "line by line" every year. Therefore, ministries have the autonomy to adjust their spending plans during the course of the year to respond to the needs on the ground quickly without seeking MOF's approval for any deviation as long as the total expenditure is within the multi-year block budget that has been determined.[n] They can also "borrow" a certain percentage of the budget for the current year from future allocations and "carry forward" budget allocations that are unused in the current year to the future for up to 3 years.

Nevertheless, under the block budget system, additional approvals are required for large development projects to ensure rigour in the cost–benefit analysis of the projects. Projects above $80 million are to be evaluated by MOF and approved by a ministerial Development Planning Committee (DPC), which comprises the Minister for Finance, Minister for Trade and Industry and the Minister of the proposing ministry. In addition, large projects with a value greater than $500 million or which are complex in nature, have to be reviewed by a Development Projects Advisory Panel (DPAP) formed by current and former senior public servants and industry experts

---

[n] The Ministry of Finance however reserves the prerogative to "subject to treasury sanction" any line item that it has objections to.

before submission to the DPC. Info-communication technology projects also need to be scrubbed by the Public Sector Infocomm Review Committee. These processes serve to ensure financial discipline in ensuring general cost norms are complied with and other approaches that may deliver the project outcomes at lower costs have been considered as alternatives before the projects proceed.

The Singapore government also seeks to meet new and emerging needs without additional funding. The growth factor provided to the block budgets of ministries is less than GDP growth so that operating revenues would grow faster than the increase in block budgets. The revenue growth which is not allocated to the ministries is set aside into a central Reinvestment Fund administered by MOF. Ministries can bid competitively for funding from the Reinvestment Fund to undertake projects and programmes meeting emerging strategic needs. The total amount available for new needs is limited by the amount available in the Reinvestment Fund, and priority of funding is given to innovative ideas that generate positive long-term spin-offs and those that promote cross-agency collaborations to address priority or new areas of need. The Reinvestment Fund therefore caters for changing spending needs in a sustainable way.

Maximising Value for Money

Under the block budget framework, the ministries do not need to return any cost savings back to the MOF but could redirect the unused budgets for new projects or initiatives without the MOF's approval. Therefore, ministries would have every incentive to improve efficiency and raise productivity and to do more with block budget that has been allocated to them.

The MOF also puts in place initiatives to help the ministries achieve greater value for money. For example, the MOF helps aggregate the purchases of public agencies which enable the agencies to enjoy savings through economies of scale and bulk purchases. This applies particularly to goods and services that are standardised or require little customisation, such as stationery, cleaning, and printing services. The MOF also helps develop partnerships with private sector experts on the design, building, and operation of assets for provision of public services. Through such long-term public–private partnerships or PPPs, the private sector could be tapped on to introduce new technology and innovative practices that reduce downstream maintenance and operating costs. The private sector could also develop new uses for the assets to generate higher revenues, thereby achieving better value for money over entire life cycles of assets. PPP has been applied to incineration plants, water treatment plants, IT services, as well as sports facilities. PPP also helps smooth out the lumpy development expenditures to develop assets needed for the delivery of public services, which the government would otherwise have to incur upfront.

The ability to extract maximum value from limited resources is not just about putting in place initiatives or programmes to cut costs and reduce budgets. It is also important to create a culture of sensible spending that involves top-down leadership and vision, as well as bottom-up involvement. Therefore, the need to achieve value for money and the initiatives to do so are integrated into all aspects of public administration and governance. Examples of such initiatives include the e-government initiative, which seeks to generate efficiencies from putting government services online and integrating the services across organisations to deliver higher productivity and improve customer satisfaction. Agencies are also required to go through value management processes when undertaking new projects of significant sizes, to ensure that the projects provide the best value for money over the life cycle of the project. The push for innovation across the civil service also created the environment for agencies to create and deliver value at lower costs to the public. In this way, the Singapore public service has been able to continually deliver better outcomes with limited fiscal resources.

Resource Management — Planning for Assets Replacement and Optimisation

Fiscal policies in most countries tend to focus on managing cash flows, that is, matching the inflows of cash from various sources of state revenues with the cash outlays. However, much of state resources are "non-cash" in nature. For example, government buildings, infrastructure, and other physical assets "accumulated" from development spending disbursed in past budgets. Without sufficient management attention, these non-cash assets would be underutilised and their upgrading or replacements not well-managed. Consequently, assets may be overbuilt or the government may not have the fiscal resources for redevelopment of the assets when needed.

The Singapore government has put in place a Resource Management framework to keep track of asset depreciation. The annual "non-cash" cost of each asset (its depreciation expenditure), which is determined by dividing the total cost of the asset against the period of its useful life, is accrued in "resource accounts" that are reported to the senior management of the agencies and to the MOF. Agencies are encouraged to generate revenues by, for example, charging fees to cover the full costs of their operations including the non-cash components, i.e. depreciation expenditures. Statutory boards which can retain their own revenues are responsible for accumulating sinking funds, borrowing, or finding funds from within existing and future budgets to finance their capital expenditures. If the assets cannot be funded from the statutory boards' operations, the agencies would have to seek the concurrence of the MOF to fund the replacement of the assets when they are due or to divest the assets to the private sector, which would be responsible for replacing the assets as and when necessary. Therefore, the asset replacements of public infrastructures and operational assets of ports, airports, industrial and housing estates, which are managed by statutory boards, are proactively planned and managed.

The MOF had experimented with "resource budgeting" at the level of government ministries and departments to artificially reproduce the environment under which statutory boards had to earn the revenues to cover their full accrued costs of operation. This involves providing the ministries with an artificial "resource budget" which is capped to match their total cash and non-cash costs. Agencies are encouraged to reduce the total costs and accumulate "profits" which could be "converted" into cash budgets to fund new operations or invest into new assets. However, due to the arbitrariness of the resource budget caps, which did not provide for new developmental plans that would provide for future needs, and the complexity introduced into the annual budget planning, resource budgeting was replaced with office space management which provided MOF with a simple and effective tool to manage the non-cash expenditures of most ministries which comprised largely office space usage. Other than office space, the major non-cash costs incurred by the government and not accounted for in the accounts of statutory boards are for large infrastructures such as road networks, and state buildings, which could be managed effectively by the processes of long-term urban and fiscal planning.

Summary

Taken together, these elements of the budgeting system — the block budgets, initiatives to maximise value for money, and resource

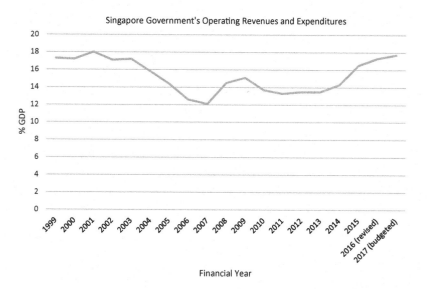

Figure 5: Singapore Government's Expenditures (1999–2017).
Source: Budget Highlights (Ministry of Finance, 2005–2017)

management — have enabled the Singapore government to sustain a low level of public spending, while improving the efficiency and effectiveness of public services to meet the ever-increasing demands of the public. The government has kept its expenditures[o] to less than 18% of GDP[51] since 1999 (see Fig. 5). By keeping a lean and small government, Singapore could sustain low taxes to provide an environment that encourages work and promotes investment.

---

[o] Excluding Land-Related Expenditures, one-off special transfers and top-ups to trust funds and endowment funds.

SECTION III

MARSHALLING ECONOMIC RESOURCES FOR PRODUCTIVE GROWTH

Chapter 11

A Pro-Enterprise and Pro-Work Fiscal Environment

As explained in Chapters 5 and 6, the policy of balancing the budget over the long term contributes to macroeconomic stability which promotes investment. To adopt a "balanced budget" policy, a government can choose to operate as either a large government that incurs high expenditures funded by high taxes or a small government with low expenditures and low taxes. The Singapore government explicitly decided to do the latter.

Small Government, Low Taxes

Singapore has chosen to keep its public expenditures low. Other than public goods that are non-excludable and non-rivalrous, such as defence and internal security, public services are largely delivered at fees charged based on full cost recovery. This policy has helped moderate the demand for public services and kept the Singapore government lean and small. Besides reducing the need to fund these services from general taxation, the public sector agencies are also held accountable for maintaining the quality and efficiency of the services which users have to pay for. Consequently, the public sector has outsourced the provision of various services such as postal services, telecommunications, and public utilities to the private sector, which is better placed and organised to deliver such services at lower costs and better quality. In fact, at one point, the Singapore government had in place a "Yellow Pages" rule, which essentially means that any service that is provided in the private sector and listed in the Yellow Pages (a directory of businesses) should not be provided by the public sector unless there are extenuating reasons to do so. An example of an extenuating reason, and therefore a justified exception for the public sector to provide the services available in the private sector, is to provide a price benchmark to keep prices low for meritorious goods which have significant positive externalities. So the Singapore government continues to be the main supplier in the housing, education, and healthcare sectors to keep prices in these areas affordable. These services are not provided for free, but the fees charged for them are affordable. The Singapore government applies a co-payment policy to ensure that the consumers bear a part of the costs involved in the provision of these services.

In the area of social transfers, the Singapore government has kept social assistance to a basic subsistence level targeted at "down-and-outs" — people who are not able to work because of disabilities and have no one else to depend on. The underlying philosophy is that the people's needs are best met through economic growth, which needs to be driven by a progressive and motivated population. The minimalist social assistance scheme is intended to strengthen the self-sufficiency and resourcefulness of the population. This is supplemented by measures to help Singaporeans stay employable by upgrading their skills, and re-equipping themselves with new skills to meet the needs of new growth industries.

In a cyclical downturn, the government also provides fiscal support to help businesses cope with labour costs so that unemployment levels are kept low.

While analysts are of the view that the Singaporean welfare model has succeeded in keeping public expenditure low and promoting a strong work ethic,[52] others have pointed out that the model also incurs social costs in terms of the inadequacy of social safety nets[53] for various growing social needs. The government has in fact strengthened social safety nets over the years. Since the 1990s, social support to lower-income households has been gradually expanded through funding provided by various endowment funds, such as EduSave, MediFund, and schemes, such as the GST Voucher and Silver Support, to provide assistance in targeted ways without eroding the work ethics of the population. In the late 1997s, the government established community development councils to administer various social assistance schemes on the ground to needy families. In 2013, the government announced the creation of social service offices to increase the number of touch points to better help the needy. Nevertheless, the safety nets are still kept small and "targeted to make a real difference to their lives, without inadvertently discouraging other able-bodied Singaporeans from making the effort to work and provide for themselves."[54] It is also worth noting that the government has continued to encourage those who have succeeded and done well to give back to society. Generous fiscal incentives are provided to encourage charitable giving in the form of deductions of up to 2.5 times the amounts donated against taxable incomes.[p] This aims to "crowd in" the rest of society to help address the various social and community needs and serve the objective of strengthening the social fabric while keeping public spending low.

Diversification of Tax Base to Keep Direct Taxes Low

In spite of the co-payment policy for public services, Singapore's ageing population is expected to lead to higher consumption of public services, especially in the healthcare sector. At the same time, as retirees leave the workforce, a shrinking tax base would drive income tax revenues down. Tax rates need to increase for the rising expenditures to be fiscally sustainable. But raising income taxes would reduce

---

[p] This will expire on 31 December 2018.

incentives for investment and employment, and exacerbate the situation further.

This problem was anticipated in the 1990s when the Singapore government introduced the GST — a tax on consumption of goods and services. GST would allow the Singapore government to diversify the tax base from income taxes. The GST rate was set at 3% when it was implemented in 1994. This was gradually raised to 4% and 5% in 2003 and 2004, respectively, and has been 7% since 2007. The implementation of GST has in fact enabled the Singapore government to reduce income tax rates as part of tax reforms undertaken in the 1990s and 2000s to enhance Singapore's attractiveness to FDI (see Fig. 6).

The implementation of GST provided the government with the fiscal space to reduce the CIT rate from 30% in 1993 progressively to 20% in 2007. PIT was also reduced from 33% to 20% (top bracket rate) over the same period.

Despite expenditure increases from 12.1% of GDP in 2007 to 14.3% in 2014, the Singapore government did not need to raise taxes

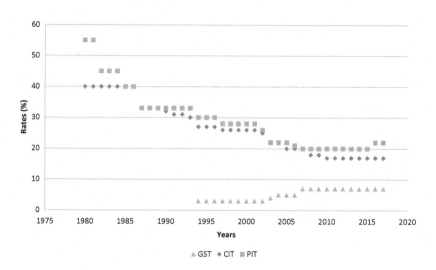

Figure 6:   Singapore Tax Rates from 1980 to 2017.

Source: Compiled by author from various sources.

and could in fact reduce CIT further to 18% in 2008 and to 17% from 2010 following the Global Financial Crisis. The government was able to do so because the constitution was amended in 2008 to allow the government to spend up to 50% of the "Expected Long-Term Real Rate of Return" on the past reserves under the NIR framework.

Public expenditures grew to 16.3% of GDP in 2015 and were projected to rise to above 17% of GDP from 2016 mainly for healthcare expenditures to address the needs of an ageing population and infrastructure enhancements to provide for a larger population. Thus, the PIT rate will be raised to 22% for the top bracket for incomes earned in 2016 to enhance the progressivity of the PIT schedule and to strengthen revenues. The government also enhanced the NIR framework in 2015 to allow it to draw more on past reserves for its operating expenditures so that direct taxes can be kept low to encourage investment and enterprise. Nevertheless, in the budget statement released in February 2017, the Minister for Finance Mr Heng Swee Keat hinted that tax increases were being considered as spending pressures build up.

Encouraging Work

PITs reduces the after-tax wages. When PITs increase, workers at the margin would ask for higher wage rates to compensate for the higher taxes. This raises wage costs, and ultimately employers may be less willing to hire more workers or even allow some workers to go. Thus, higher taxes can discourage employment.

The shift from direct taxes to GST allowed the Singapore government to raise revenues without significant increases in PITs. However, by taxing consumption, lower-income households who consume a larger proportion of their incomes would pay more taxes as a percentage of their income.

The implementation of GST in 1994 was therefore supplemented by both one-off and permanent transfers, including increased subsidies for healthcare, education, and housing to offset increases in costs of living, especially for lower-income households so that taking into account benefits received, higher-income households continue to pay the bulk of taxes on a net basis, whereas lower-income households receive permanent benefits exceeding total taxes paid.

The Workfare Income Supplement (WIS) scheme was one of the permanent transfers schemes put in place when GST was last raised in 2007. The WIS scheme encourages low-wage workers to stay employed and nudge the low-skill unemployed back to the workforce by supplementing their pay. The scheme is complemented by the Workfare Training Support (WTS) scheme implemented in 2010 which provides incentives for low-wage workers to go for training and upgrade their skills. The aim of WTS scheme is to help low-wage workers eventually graduate out of the WIS scheme. Broad-based transfers for continuous education and training (CET) are also provided to subsidise the training expenditures for adult learning and skills upgrading. These schemes, which have been enhanced over the years, are designed to encourage self-reliance and work so that Singaporeans see sustained welfare improvements through employment and upgrading of skills to earn higher incomes. The creation of a pro-enterprise fiscal environment that enables Singapore to continue attracting investments in turn creates good jobs that Singaporeans can undertake.

Encouraging Investments and Enterprise

To promote a pro-business environment, the government not only maintains a low CIT but also offers additional incentives such as the development and expansion incentive which provides a reduced corporate tax rate of 5% or 10% on incremental income from significant capital expenditures and business spending that leads to development of skilled jobs or the anchoring of leading-edge technology, skills, or activities in Singapore. Other tax incentives are also provided to encourage the development of high value economic activities in Singapore. These include the following:

— Grants under the Research Incentive Scheme for Companies (RISC) for companies to develop R&D capabilities in strategic areas of technology;

Helping Small and Medium Enterprises Upgrade

In addition to the Productivity and Innovation Credit (PIC) Scheme and tax incentives for R&D expenditures, SMEs which have an annual turnover of less than $100 million or less than 200 employees can apply for the Capability Development Grant to defray up to 70% of qualifying project costs (e.g., consultancy, training, certification, equipment, and software costs) that contribute to raising productivity, process improvement, product development, and market access. These SMEs can also use Innovation and Capability Vouchers of up to $5,000 to redeem R&D related services from service providers to upgrade operations.

To enable SMEs to participate in the supply chains of large companies, selected SMEs are given fiscal support under the Partnerships for Capability Transformation Scheme to improve productivity and develop the capabilities needed to meet the qualification criteria imposed by large companies for their suppliers. SMEs are also provided funding support under the Collaborative Industry Projects Scheme to collaborate and work with trade associations and solution providers to raise productivity through projects such as shared services or co-exploration of market opportunities.

To encourage local businesses to internationalise, a Double Tax Deduction for Internationalisation Scheme is provided to offset the expenses incurred by local businesses in areas such as overseas development trips, study trips, overseas trade fairs, and expenses of employees posted overseas to develop overseas market access.

— Finance & Treasury Centre (FTC) tax incentive to provide a reduced corporate tax rate of 8% on fees, interest, and gains from qualifying services and activities for a specified period of time. It also provides a withholding tax exemption on interest payments on loans from non-resident banks as well as loans and deposits from non-resident approved network companies, for FTC activities;

— International Headquarters (IHQ) Award which provides a reduced corporate tax rate of 5% or 10% on incremental income from substantive global headquarters activities carried out in Singapore; and

— Aircraft Leasing Scheme (ALS) to provide a reduced corporate tax rate on income accruing in or derived from Singapore from leasing of aircraft or aircraft engine and prescribed activities. It also provides automatic withholding tax exemption on qualifying payments on qualifying foreign loans for the purchase of aircraft or aircraft engines.

The Singapore government promotes market competition so that only businesses that are efficient and productive can grow. While inefficient and loss making operations would fold up and lead to a temporary increase in unemployment, resources could be redeployed to other profit making and higher-value businesses or industries. The provision of tax incentives is the most effective fiscal tool that targets financial support to businesses that are profitable since the incentives can only be realised if the businesses record chargeable incomes. To encourage the growth of new businesses, a Start-Up Tax Exemption scheme provides full tax exemption on the first $100,000 of chargeable income and 50% tax exemption on the next $200,000 of chargeable income for first there consecutive years. In addition, all companies who do not qualify for the tax exemption scheme for new start-ups can enjoy a 75% tax exemption on the first $10,000 of chargeable income and a further 50% tax exemption on the next $290,000 of chargeable income. These schemes significantly reduce the effective corporate tax rates for start-ups and SMEs.

The Singapore government also provides grants and tax reliefs on investments made by businesses to undertake productivity enhancing activities, such as research and staff training. For example, under the Productivity and Innovation Credit (PIC) scheme, businesses will qualify for 400% tax deductions for expenditures up to $400,000 incurred for training of employees, R&D, investment in design projections acquisition and licensing of intellectual property rights, acquisition and leasing of information technology and automation equipment from 2011 to 2018. Beyond the $400,000 cap, a 150% tax deduction is provided for R&D activities undertaken in Singapore.

Expenditures on R&D done overseas will enjoy a lower 100% tax deduction. These and other fiscal subsidies serve to help businesses improve efficiency, lower costs, and become more competitive over the long run.

Other than the low CITs, exports and transshipment goods are effectively tax-free. Imports are largely subject only to the GST, while exports are zero-rated for GST.[q] In addition, incomes from financial investments, including capital gains on properties and financial investments, dividend income earned by holders of Singapore resident company shares and unit trusts, and interest income on bank fixed deposits, are exempt from tax. These attributes of the tax regime enable the Singapore economy to function as a competitive and efficient market with minimal price distortions caused by taxes. They have also contributed to the city state's development as a global and regional hub for trade and finance, export, and transshipment.

Addressing the Negative Externalities of Businesses

Fiscal tools are also deployed to supplement regulation in the management of negative externalities produced by economic activities. For example, taxes are imposed on tobacco and alcohol products to deter their consumption because of health concerns. To address road congestion, high taxes are levied on vehicle ownership to control the growth in vehicle population in addition to road tolls to discourage usage of vehicles during peak periods. Petrol and diesel taxes are also imposed so that vehicle owners economise on their usage, which contributes to air pollution. The government also introduced a carbon tax in Budget 2017 to encourage businesses and households to reduce energy consumption from sources emitting greenhouse gases.

By moderating the production and consumption of products and services with negative externalities through the use of fiscal levers, the

---

[q] Import duties are limited to liquor and tobacco products and motor vehicles.

economy has been able to generate net positive benefits to stakeholders. This has contributed to making Singapore a conducive place for investors as well as talents from around the world.

Summary

The introduction of GST along with schemes to alleviate the impact on lower-income households has enabled Singapore to diversify its tax system away from income taxes. Consequently, PIT and CIT rates have been reduced to encourage work, entreprise, and investment. Supplemented by a small and lean government, investment incomes from past reserves, and a pro-business tax regime, Singapore has created a pro-enterprise fiscal environment to sustain Singapore's economic growth over the years.

Chapter 12

Optimise Usage of Limited Land Resources

Besides keeping taxes low, government intervention and regulation in Singapore is limited to the necessary so that market players can respond nimbly to new opportunities. Generally, the market is allowed to work through price signals so that scarce resources can be deployed quickly to wherever there is demand for them. The Singapore government selectively influences the market to achieve its goal to create jobs and raise incomes for Singaporeans through the fiscal levers of tax reliefs and incentives to promote innovation, stimulate entrepreneurship, and encourage firms to raise productivity and support worker training. Grants and subsidies are supplemented by foreign worker levies imposed on employers to reduce their reliance on low-cost foreign workers.

Nevertheless, the Singapore government intervenes strongly beyond taxes and subsidies when there are extenuating circumstances to do so. One area where it does so is in the management of land supply.

In larger countries, free markets determine the rise and fall of cities. For example, the "Manufacturing Belt" states in the Midwest of the United States grew in importance with the growth of industrial manufacturing after World War II. Cities in these states flourished because of their connectivity to consumer markets as well as proximity to raw material sources such as iron mines. These cities also had the capacity to accommodate migrant workers who provided the labor needed for industrial growth. As the US economy restructured, economic activities shifted to new cities in the "Sun Belt" such as Texas, San Francisco, Florida, and South and North Carolina, which are more liveable (warmer) and where new economic opportunities emerged. The Manufacturing Belt became known as the "Rust Belt". Nevertheless, the US as a country continued to grow at the aggregate level as new cities contributed to economic growth that offset the declines in other cities. Cities that had declined could be also rejuvenated. For example, Pittsburgh, which is located in the Rust Belt, experienced a revival brought about by the growth of medical and business services.

The sprawl of the US, coupled with the free movement of labour and capital, and openness to global talent, allows its cities to develop and rejuvenate organically in response to changes. But in the case of Singapore, which has a land area of only about 700 square kilometers, or less than half the size of London, the supply of land is managed carefully to ensure that current and future needs of the city state are well provided for, and the economy can constantly reinvent itself to serve new niches in the global market. Unlike other global cities which are one of many cities within a large country, Singapore's land use has to provide for all the needs of a country including military bases and other infrastructures that serve national functions.

Currently, more than 90% of land in Singapore is state-owned[55], and much of real estate in Singapore is built on land leased from the state. This unique situation was enabled by the Land Acquisition Act enacted in 1966 which empowered the Singapore government to acquire land for public purposes by paying for the land based on current use. For example, when rural land was acquired, compensation was based on the value of the land based on farm use even if the Singapore government intended to develop the land for residential or industrial purposes. Between 1973 and 1987, the compensation paid for the land acquired by Singapore government was based on market rates as of 30 November 1973 or the date of acquisition, whichever was lower. Ownership of land in Singapore grew from 44% in 1960 to 76% in 1985. From 1987, the Land Acquisition Act was amended to peg compensation at current market rates. The state also reclaims land from the sea to add to its land bank. Over the years, the land area of Singapore has grown from 582 square kilometers in 1965[56] to 719 square kilometers in 2016.[57]

Land is sold by the Singapore government to private developers with leases up to 99 years for specific purposes, such as housing, commercial, or industrial purposes (in a small number of cases the land is sold without specified uses to allow the private sector developer to respond to market needs). Land is also alienated to statutory boards such as the JTC and HDB for development. Ownership reverts to the Singapore government at the end of the leases, enabling the Singapore government to release the land for redevelopment to serve changing needs. The uses are determined in accordance to a Master Plan developed by the Urban Redevelopment Authority (URA) of Singapore, based on projections of commercial, industrial, and population needs over the next 10–15 years, reviewed every 5 years. The Master Plan is in turn derived from a Concept Plan developed for 40–50 years into the future, reviewed every 10 years.

One would expect that as the Singapore government is the largest holder of land, land revenues would comprise a significant proportion of the government's operating revenues. This is not the case. Land sales revenue is not added to the operating revenues of the government for spending but is added to the government's past reserves. In land scarce Singapore, land is considered a strategic resource that is "protected" under the Past Reserves Protection framework. Under the framework, land must be sold at fair market values and the proceeds from land sales cannot be spent in the annual budget. Correspondingly, land-related expenditures, which include expenditures incurred in reclaiming land from the sea and for land acquisition, are funded not from the government's annual budget but from the past reserves. The rationale is that these expenditures add to the land bank of the state, which forms part of past reserves.

The policy to not include land sales revenue for spending addresses two issues. One, land prices usually track underlying properties to be built on the land. Property and land prices are volatile because they are subject to interest rate changes and a certain amount of speculative demand on top of actual demand driven by fundamentals. If the Singapore government depended on such volatile and unpredictable revenue sources, the resultant budgetary uncertainty would make it difficult for the government to implement a balanced budget policy over its term. Two, the government may be tempted to "push" the sales of land to generate the revenues to sustain high expenditures. This may lead to an oversupply of land in the market, which may crash property prices with contagion downstream effects on the banking sector and the real economy.

A government land sales programme is undertaken in line with URA's Concept and Master plans to serve the long-term developmental needs of the nation. Land for various purposes (residential, industrial, or commercial) is released for sale in accordance with the implementation of the Concept and Master plans which are based on projected economic growth and demographics. The pace of land sales also takes into account property cycles. When land and property prices rise above trend, the government would bring forward the schedule of land sales to meet the high demand. This achieves a countercyclical effect by removing excess liquidity from the market to moderate land and property price increases.

On the downside of a property cycle, the government would continue to push land out to the market but in moderation and with an eye on the market prices. Land would be placed in a "reserve list" with a stated minimum price to test the market. The land would be activated for sale only when enough developers indicate interest by submitting a bid close to the price signaled as acceptable by the government. The reserve list system also ensures a continual supply of land to meet long-term development needs while maintaining a floor for land prices.

The Singapore government also continues to undertake land acquisition to rejuvenate residential and industrial estates and improve land productivity based on the Concept and Master plans. For example, older housing estates are acquired under a Selective En-bloc Redevelopment scheme for redevelopment into newer estates with higher gross plot ratios. When the government announced in May 2015 that the Kuala Lumpur–Singapore High Speed Rail terminus will be located at the site of the Jurong Country Club, it also announced that the site and its surrounding areas would be acquired for comprehensive redevelopment so that higher-value mixed-use developments and community facilities could be introduced to the areas around the terminus.

Fiscal incentives are also provided to encourage businesses to initiate projects to improve land productivity. To promote the intensification of industrial land use towards more land-efficient and higher-value-added activities, businesses in industry sectors which have large land takes and low built up areas can qualify for a one-off 25% Land Intensification Allowance (LIA) on capital expenditures incurred for the construction or renovation and extension of a qualifying building or structure. In addition, a tax allowance of 5% on the qualifying capital expenditure is provided annually until the allowances accumulate to 100%. Companies which are interested to optimise land use through domestic or overseas relocation can also qualify for the Land Productivity Grant to defray one-time, non-capital expenses related to the relocation.

Summary

In land scarce Singapore, government intervention in the management of land supply is crucial to the city state's ability to continually reinvent itself to sustain economic growth and improvements in living standards. By not taking land revenues into operating revenues for spending, land is managed optimally as a strategic asset, instead of a revenue source. Spending on development of the land bank through land acquisition and land reclamation is also charged to past reserves rather than the annual budgets. In this way, the government would not be constrained by operating revenues when it needs to make large lumpy investments for long-term land planning.

Chapter 13

Efficient Infrastructure that Supports Growth

Left to the market, public infrastructure would be underinvested because of the high outlays at the outset, the uncertainty of financial returns from the investments, and the long time taken to reap them if any, especially in nascent sectors that the government is seeking to grow. Therefore, the Singapore government is the key supplier of most strategic public infrastructure. Statutory boards are set up to ensure that the infrastructures are efficiently managed and generate revenues that pay for themselves so that the costs of the infrastructural developments do not unnecessarily add to fiscal demands.

Industrial Infrastructure

JTC was first set up in 1968 to take over from EDB which was then overseeing the development of industrial parks to host the factories of MNCs to kick-start Singapore's industrialisation efforts. Land was alienated to JTC who would develop industrial parks with loans provided by the government in the earlier years of independence. JTC would in turn sub-lease the developed industrial spaces to MNCs and local SMEs in return for rental and lease revenues that would enable JTC to finance its loans. Subsequently, when the bond market was more developed, JTC issued bonds to raise funds for the developments. This requirement for JTC to be self-financing has driven JTC to ensure that its industrial properties are well-designed to meet the needs of its users.

JTC's ability to develop financially viable industrial parks and estates was market tested when JTC divested its general-use industrial estates to private owners and operators in 2008 and 2011 at a profit over historical costs.[58] The divestment of the general-use industrial estates allowed JTC to focus on developing specialised infrastructures to support new higher-value economic clusters. These infrastructures, which include the Jurong Island for energy and chemical companies, the Biopolis for biomedical research institutes, and the Seletar Aerospace Park for the aerospace cluster, continue to be operated on a self-sustaining basis by JTC. To ensure that the infrastructures are in line with Singapore's economic strategies, JTC works closely with the EDB, which is responsible for bringing foreign companies to invest in Singapore. Both JTC and EDB report to the Ministry of Trade and Industry which sets Singapore's industrial policies.

Port Infrastructure

Singapore has always been a shipping hub by virtue of its strategic geographical location. Transshipment volumes have been driven by growth over the years in tandem with global trade as well technological advances, such as the development of steam ships and containerisation of cargo, which vastly improved the productivity of shipping and port operations.

The Harbour Board was formed to develop and manage the Singapore port under the British colonial government. After Singapore gained self-government from Britain, the government established the Port Authority of Singapore (PSA) to replace the Harbour Board to become the central agency responsible for managing and developing the ports of Singapore. PSA undertook expansion of the port infrastructure, including the establishment of Jurong Port in 1965 to support the Jurong Industrial Estate and the conversion of the British naval base into the Sembawang Shipyard in 1971. The first container berth at Tanjong Pagar was developed and operationalised in 1972. PSA financed its port operations with revenues collected from users as port dues and fees for various port services.

PSA continually expanded port infrastructures and invested in modern technology such as computerisation and automation that enhanced operational productivity. By 1988, Singapore became the world's busiest shipping port, the second-largest container port and the top bunkering port. PSA was corporatised on 1 October 1997 and renamed PSA Corporation to further ensure that Singapore's port remained responsive to developments and needs of the shipping industry in the face of increasing global competition. The regulatory functions undertaken then by PSA were taken over by the Maritime and Port Authority of Singapore (MPA). PSA and MPA work closely to continually review the need for new infrastructure to ensure the efficiency and competitiveness of Singapore's ports.

Airport Infrastructure

Air services play an important role in Singapore's economy by supporting the flow of trade, investment, and tourism. With the development of general aviation, Singapore's three civilian airports built in the urban areas of Paya Lebar, Seletar, and Kallang in the 1960s and 1970s could not cope with the passenger numbers (Passenger traffic jumped from some 600,000 in 1965 to around 4 million by 1975[59]). To cope with the accelerating demand for air travel, the Changi International Airport was developed at the coastal area of the island. The development of Changi Airport enabled the airport operations to be consolidated from the urban areas, therefore freeing the land for city redevelopment. The location at Changi also provided for future growth in air traffic through reclamation of land from the surrounding sea.

After the first terminal of Changi Airport became operational in 1981, the Department of Civil Aviation (which had been responsible for the operations of the airport) was converted into a statutory board known as the Civil Aviation Authority of Singapore (CAAS) in 1984. The CAAS became fully responsible for meeting its financial obligations in maintaining and operating Changi Airport with fees and charges collected from airlines and other users. The second terminal of Changi Airport was developed in 1990, ahead of projected growth in air traffic. Changi Airport was subsequently corporatised in 2009 and managed by Changi Airport Group, a private company fully owned by the government which also invests in and manages airports around the world. At the same time, CAAS was restructured to focus on its roles as the regulatory authority for civil aviation in Singapore and promoter of the air hub and aviation industry. The airport now has four terminals and a budget air terminal. Changi Airport is now ranked among the best and largest airports in the world. The efficiency of the airport infrastructure is important for manufacturers who need to air freight their products world-wide. It is also key for business service providers who base their headquarters or core management team in Singapore to serve the region.

Application of Market Discipline

In the first few years after Singapore's independence, the development of large infrastructures was financed by loans mainly because of fiscal constraints. These statutory boards were made responsible for ensuring that revenues generated from the developments could repay the borrowings.

Despite the availability of budget surpluses since the late 1960s, the Singapore government has continued to impose the discipline of requiring these statutory boards to finance their developments with loans from the market as much as possible. This serves a few purposes. Firstly, requiring statutory boards to borrow contributes to the development of the bond market. This also mops up access liquidity in savings surplus Singapore. Secondly, the existence of debt imposes market discipline on the statutory board to ensure the bankability of their assets. Every statutory board has to borrow at interest rates reflecting the market's assessment of the statutory board's ability to finance the debts. This creates an awareness of the cost of funds within each statutory board so that it would not develop and accumulate more assets than necessary. The financial discipline imposed on statutory boards has enabled some of them to divest the assets so that they are operated fully by corporates on a commercial basis, enabling the statutory boards to focus on their regulatory roles to deliver public policy outcomes.

Public–Private Partnerships (PPPs)

PPPs are arrangements under which the private sector participates in the provision of public services by developing, owning, and operating infrastructural assets to provide services for the public sector in return for annual payments. The most common PPP projects in Singapore are in the water sector. The government would typically enter into a user agreement with the private sector developer for the use of a water treatment plant which would be funded, constructed, and operated by the developer. The government would pay the private sector partner for the supply of water over the life span of the plant according to pre-agreed formulas.

The Next-Generation National Broadband Network (NGNBN) is another example of PPP. The Singapore government adopted PPP to leverage on the existing passive infrastructure assets, such as ducts, manholes, and exchanges owned by the private sector, as well as its operational expertise to roll out the NGNBN efficiently. Under the arrangement, a private sector consortium developed and operates the NGNBN. The consortium earns its revenues from telecommunication companies that tap on the NGNBN to provide high-speed broadband services to end-users for a fee. In addition, the government provided a grant of US$2 billion to the consortium to extend the network island wide and ensure that the network is priced affordably.[60]

Besides tapping on the assets and expertise of the private sector, PPPs also enable the Singapore government to tap on private funds for upfront investments. For example, in the redevelopment of the National Stadium into a sports hub, the $1.3 billion infrastructure was largely funded upfront by the private consortium which built it.

Under the contract, the consortium has the responsibility of maintaining the stadium with revenues earned by organising sporting events. Compared to the public sector, the private sector is also better at bringing in quality events from around the world to promote the development of a vibrant sporting sector in Singapore.

Providing for Social Infrastructure

In an export economy like Singapore, demand for economic infrastructure such as industrial estates, ports, and airports are largely international. When the infrastructures reach their limits, international users would look for alternatives in other parts of the region. The cost of not meeting the demand is lost opportunities for economic growth. However, unmet demand for domestic infrastructure meeting social needs such as housing, healthcare, and public transport affects the population directly. Besides economic costs in terms of loss of attractiveness to international talent and investors arising from a lower quality of life in the city state, the resulting crowdedness also creates social externalities such as stress and reduced sense of well-being among the population.

Through the Master and Concept plans developed by URA, which are reviewed regularly, long-term population trends such as migration and birth rates, demographic changes such as ageing, and evolving family structures such as decreasing sizes of households are built into social infrastructure development plans. To ensure responsiveness to unanticipated fluctuations in demand, the government takes on additional capital costs to build ahead of demand and bear the risks of redundancy. The government intervenes strongly to ensure not just the availability of the social infrastructure but also that prices are affordable and quality is assured. Though it would not be possible to pass on the full costs of social infrastructures to users, public and private agencies are made responsible for operating the infrastructure as efficiently as possible to keep costs low. For example, while the government continues to be responsible for the building of new hospitals, the hospitals are operated by national healthcare providers (fully owned by the government) which are held accountable

Government Role in Public Transport Infrastructure

Under a framework implemented with effect from 2016, public bus services are undertaken by private contractors appointed through competitive tendering. Public bus routes, service standards and fares are determined by the Government. Operators who are awarded the contracts will be paid fees to operate the services, while fare revenues will be retained by the Government. Under the framework, the Government will own all bus infrastructure, such as depots, as well as operating assets such as buses and the fleet management system to lower the barriers of entry to the market, and attract more bus operators to bring down the costs of operations and raise efficiency. Compared to the private sector, the Government is more prepared to build the bus infrastructure ahead of time to cater for anticipated increases in demand or to raise service standards.

For rail services, the Government similarly owns the rail infrastructure such as stations and depots as well as operating assets such as the trains and signaling system, and makes the decisions to build up, replace or upgrade these assets to respond to growing ridership and commuter expectations. Rail operators are appointed based on competition to operate the rail services and maintain the trains. The rail operator shares in the revenues from operating the lines but have to pay a Licence Charge, pegged to the operator's profits, which is set aside for upgrading of the rail infrastructure in due course.

for recovering the operational costs of the hospitals. The hospitals charge fees based on full costs which are reduced for patients who qualify for subsidies provided by the government for specified treatments and different types of wards. Competition among the hospitals for patients provides the incentive for the hospitals to keep costs low and make available medical services to the public at affordable prices. Similarly, while the government builds the infrastructure for public transport, competition among transport operators for the right to deliver public transport services helps keep costs and fares low.

The government also experimented with a Design, Build and Sell Scheme (DBSS) for public housing in 2005 to allow private developers to participate in the development of public housing. The developers were allowed to bid competitively for land to sell to Singaporeans who qualified to purchase public housing directly from HDB. The buyers were able to utilise the housing grants provided by the government to offset the sales prices of the DBSS flats. The intent of DBSS was to introduce better designs into public housing and enable the market to take over from the government the risks of unsold flats. However, on the upswing of the property cycle, developers took the opportunity to set high prices for the DBSS flats which led to concerns over profiteering. The government eventually decided to suspend the DBSS in 2011. HDB continues to be the major developer of new public housing, raising funds from the bond market for the development of new flats, which are sold to the public at a discount. The loss incurred by HDB on each flat is funded directly by the government upon the sale of the flat. HDB keeps the costs low by outsourcing the construction to companies which are appointed based on competitive bidding.

While subsidies are generally provided by the government for social infrastructure such as healthcare, transport, and public transport to keep their costs affordable for the public, water infrastructure is fully priced to reflect its long-run marginal cost, that is, the cost of producing the next drop of potable water. A tiered water tariff is charged so that heavy users pay a higher rate. A water conservation tax, which is calculated as a percentage of total water consumption, is also imposed on the user. The differentiated water tariff and conservation tax serve to discourage excessive water consumption in water-starved Singapore. In addition, water users pay a monthly sanitary appliance fee and waterborne fee to offset the cost of treating used water and for the operation and maintenance of the public sewer system.

Summary

The Singapore government plays a leading role in the planning and development of key economic infrastructures such as industrial estates, ports, and airports in line with national economic strategies. Nevertheless, these infrastructures are operated by statutory boards or corporate entities on a self-financing basis. Market discipline is applied on the entities which are required to raise debt, as far as it is possible, for the development or upgrading of the infrastructures and to finance the debts subsequently with the revenues from operating the infrastructures. Where the private sector is better placed to build, own, and operate the infrastructure, the government would also enter into PPPs for the operation of the infrastructure. While operators of social infrastructures such as hospitals and public transport are not responsible for recovering the full costs of the infrastructures directly from users, the costs of maintaining and operating the infrastructures are similarly kept low with the similar imposition of financial accountability on public and private operators of the infrastructures. This has enabled the government to minimise the capital expenditures as well as subsidies to build and keep the infrastructures running.

Chapter 14

Regulating the Inflow of Foreign Workers

Singapore had always had an open labour market policy. In the earlier part of the 1800s, the free movement of people from Malaysia and other parts of Southeast Asia to and from Singapore were the main drivers of the population changes in Singapore. Chinese immigrants also started coming into Singapore in large numbers soon after China lost the Opium War and treaty ports were given to Britain (as well as France, Germany, and Japan) from which Chinese could board ships to the South Seas (or "Nanyang" in Chinese). Many of them came through Singapore which was a shipping hub for the region. These were mainly transient workers who would stay in Singapore as long as there were jobs, but they would also leave for better prospects in other parts of the region.[61]

When Singapore became independent, the status of its resident population changed overnight from migrants to citizens. The Singapore government became responsible for taking care of their welfare if they had no jobs. Unemployment in 1959 was as high as 13.5% and projected to get worse. Fiscal resources were invested in infrastructure development and tax incentives given to encourage private sector investments to grow the economy to provide jobs for the people. To ensure that the industrialisation of Singapore benefited its citizens, the Regulation of Employment Act was enacted in 1965 to control the number of foreign workers. Foreigners could work in Singapore only with permits that were applied on their behalf by employers. The policies were so successful in reducing unemployment by the 1970s that Singapore had since then allowed a continual inflow of foreign works to sustain the growth of the economy.

To encourage higher-value companies to set up operations in Singapore, the government initially granted the companies free access to any grade of labour from any part of the world. Work permits for lower-skill labour were granted freely. Malaysia was the main source of foreign workers at the beginning, but this soon had to be supplemented by "non-traditional" sources such as Bangladesh and Thailand. At the same time, the government embarked on initiatives to restructure the manufacturing sector with a two-prong approach. On the one hand, tax incentives were shifted towards higher-value and more capital-intensive sectors. On the other hand, the government invested in upgrading the skills of the workforce. In 1979, the Skills Development Fund was established to finance the training of employees, retrain retrenched workers, and upgrade business operations and technology. This is funded by a Skills Development Levy, which is payable by businesses at 0.25% of the monthly remuneration for each employee, with a cap for employees earning above a certain salary (currently set at $4,500 a month). The levy was intended to nudge businesses to invest in improving their work processes and training of staff to reduce reliance on low-cost labour.

The number of foreign workers as a percentage of the workforce grew from 3.2% in 1970 to 7.4% in 1980.[62] Cognizant of the costs on infrastructure and concerned that the influx of cheap foreign labour would suppress the wages of Singaporean workers, administrative measures were put in place to limit the number of industries that could employ foreign workers, with the implementation of Dependent Ratio Ceilings (ratio of foreign to local workers) for employers in approved industries. The Foreign Worker Levy (FWL) was introduced in 1982 as a price-based mechanism to regulate the inflow of low-skill foreign workers. Because employers were required to make contributions to the CPF for Singaporean workers, foreign workers had been relatively cheaper. The FWL was thus set at 30% of the wages of foreign workers, above the employer's 25% contribution to CPF for local workers. This served to discourage employers from indiscriminate recruitment of cheaper low-skill foreign workers, which reduced the need for businesses to upgrade through automation and mechanisation. While the Dependency Ratio Ceilings ensure a Singaporean core in the workforces of businesses, the price mechanism of the FWL allocates the supply of foreign labour to high-value and growing industries that could afford the levies but suffered from labour shortages.

The government's initial intent announced in 1981 was to phase out unskilled labour from non-traditional sources by 1986 and from traditional sources (primarily Malaysia) by 1991. But because of the slow growth in the local workforce, the tight labour market remained a constraint for businesses, both MNCs as well as local SMEs, seeking to grow. Following the 1985 recession, the government recognised that Singapore industries needed to have access to foreign workers to grow, especially to overcome temporary shortages and to work in jobs where it was difficult to employ Singaporeans. In 1992, a two-tier levy was implemented such that the levy for a semi-skilled worker is lower than that for an unskilled worker to encourage employers to employ higher skilled workers.[63] The dependency ratios were raised over time, but higher levy rates were imposed for employers who hired a larger number of foreign workers relative to their workforces. This enhanced the flexibility for competitive businesses to access additional foreign workers to grow on the upturn of business cycles.

During the period from 2012 to 2016, around 70% of the foreign workforce (excluding foreign domestic workers) were low-skill work permit holders. The other 30% comprised "S" pass holders and employment pass holders. "S" pass holders are "mid-level skilled" workers such as technicians and service staff. The FWL is also applicable on each "S" pass granted to employers, and the number of such middle-skill workers employed by an employer is also limited by dependency ratios. Employment pass holders are high-skill foreigners with acceptable degrees or specialist skills earning incomes above levels specified by the Ministry of Manpower. While low- and middle-skill foreign workers are regulated, high-skill foreigners are welcomed. The FWL and dependency ratios are not applicable on the employers of these foreign professionals, managers, and executives. The rationale is that these skilled foreigners serve to meet the demand for professional and specialist skillsets lacking in the local workforce, which are needed to move the economy into higher-value activities. The high-skill foreign workforce also contributes to transfer of knowledge to local workers.

Foreign Workers as Buffers against Job Losses

The use of FWL as a regulator of foreign labour has allowed foreign workers, especially low-skill ones, to fill job vacancies and allow employers to keep costs low to stay competitive internationally. This has enabled the Singapore economy to capitalise on growth opportunities on the upturn of economic cycles and create jobs for Singaporeans.

On the other hand, when the economy goes through a downturn, the foreign workforce buffers local workers from large job losses. According to a study by the Ministry of Manpower,[64] the bulk of the job losses in manufacturing from 1998 to 2003 were borne by foreign workers, whereas 9 out of 10 jobs created, mainly in the services sector, went to the local workforce. In the decade that followed from 2004 to 2015, between 8,500 and 15,580 workers were displaced every year.[65] Over the period, foreign workers (excluding foreign domestic workers) made up a disproportionately larger share of the displaced workers than the ratios of the workforce that the foreign worker comprised (see Fig. 7 reconstructed based on findings from the study).

Tightening of Foreign Labour

The Singapore government has continually tightened the foreign labour inflow by raising the FWL to prompt businesses to economise on the use of labour. When the FWL scheme was introduced in 1982, employers were required to pay a monthly levy of 30% of the monthly

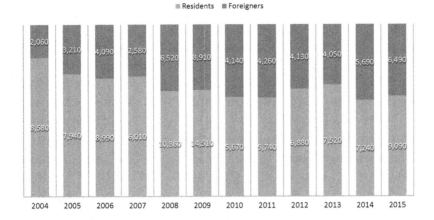

Figure 7: Redundancy by Residential Status (2004–2015).

Source: "Redundancy and Re-entry into Employment 2015" (Manpower Research and Statistics Department, April 2016).

wages of their foreign workers, subject to a minimum of $150 per month. From 1 July 2016, levies up to $950 per worker have been imposed, depending on the sector, the worker's qualifications or skills, and the dependency ratios. In general, the employer would have to pay higher levies if he employs more foreign workers relative to local employees, but the levies would be moderated if the foreign workers were higher skilled. The levies would also be higher for sectors where the government saw a greater need for automation and productivity improvements, such as in the construction sector.

The increases in FWL have generally been done with an eye on their impact on businesses. On an upturn of the economy, the growth of business activities would usually be accompanied by an increase in employment of foreign workers. The higher FWL collection by the government in turn helps prevent overheating of the economy. The FWL therefore acts as an automatic fiscal stabiliser as the economy grows. In fact, the government usually takes the opportunity of good economic growth to further increase levies. On the other hand, the reduction of employment leads to lower FWL collections during a downturn. The government would consider reducing the levy rates in the event of a downturn and when the number of foreign workers fall. For example, the levy for skilled work permit holders was reduced to help businesses tide over the downturn in 1998 and 1999. The percentage of foreign workers in the workforce fell from 30.8% in 1998 to around 28.1% in 2003 as economic growth slowed. As the economy picked up and the share of foreign workers as a percentage of the total labour force began to rise to 28.9% in 2005, the government progressively raised the levy. In spite of increases in levy rates, the share of foreign workers continued to grow to 34.7% in 2010. The government has since then resisted pressures to reduce the FWL even on the downturn of the economy and kept largely to a path of raising the levies to keep the share of foreign workers in the workforce to around one-third. Consequently, the foreign workforce growth rate has moderated from 11% during 2006–2010 (4 years) to around 5% per annum during 2010–2015 (5 years). In fact, foreign employment (excluding foreign domestic workers) contracted for the first time since 2009 in 2016 by 0.2% while local employment continued growing (see Table 4) even as the economy grew at only 2%, the slowest since 2010. Foreign workers made up 33.6% of the workforce in 2016, down from 2010.

Planned FWL increases were postponed in 2016 and 2017 for sectors such as the marine and process sectors which were facing challenging business conditions and where the number of foreign workers was declining. The government proceeded with the foreign worker levy hikes for the construction sector notwithstanding the slowdown in construction activities, but this was supplemented with support measures such as a $150 million Public Sector Construction Productivity Fund and the bringing forward of $700 million worth of public sector infrastructure projects to start in 2017 and 2018.

Table 4:   Year-on-Year Percentage Change in Employment by Residential Status.

	2010	2011	2012	2013	2014	2015	2016#
Local	2.9	1.9	2.9	4.0	4.4	0.0	0.5
Foreign*	6.3	8.8	6.8	4.6	2.4	2.0	−0.2

*excluding foreign domestic workers, # provisional numbers
Source: Labour Market Advance Release 2016 (Manpower Research and Statistics Department).

Raising Productivity

While the FWL has been raised to tighten the inflow of low-skill foreign workers, the Singapore government has provided more fiscal incentives such as tax deductions and grants to help businesses increase productivity through automation and innovation, especially in sectors such as the construction, hospitality, and healthcare sectors, which generally found it difficult to recruit local workers. Substantial support is also provided to help workers improve their productivity and skills so that they stay employable and earn higher incomes as businesses restructure. In this way, higher FWL collections arising from higher FWL rates are recycled back to businesses who invest in raising productivity. But businesses who do not do so will experience a net tax increase. Over time, the businesses who are not able to transform and be competitive enough to pay higher FWL rates would have to relocate out of Singapore to a lower-cost location or close down.

As the Singapore government's efforts to structure the economy took fruit from 2004 to 2007, jobs created in the services sector, which were filled mainly by local workers, exceeded the jobs lost by locals. This brought resident unemployment down from 4.1% in 2004 and 2005 to 3.0% in 2007. Although unemployment worsened briefly to 3.2% in 2008 and 4.3% in 2009 because of the Global Financial Crisis, the government's measures to help businesses tide through the crisis and to train local workers enabled the Singapore economy to capitalise on the rebound in global activity to grow stronger the following year. Resident unemployment also recovered to 3.1%. Since then, resident unemployment was kept at 3% or lower as the government continued to tighten the inflow of foreign workers to encourage companies to invest in productivity improvements. In addition, initiatives to help the local workforce upskill and stay employed, such as various training programmes funded by the government, Place and Train schemes, and workfare, have contributed to keeping Singapore's unemployment to lower than the levels in advanced countries such as the US, Japan, and Germany from the 1990s till now (see Table 5).

Table 5: Unemployment Rates in the US, Japan, Germany, Organisation for Economic Co-operation and Development (OECD) compared with Singapore Total and Resident Unemployment Rates.

Country	1980	1985	1990	1995	2000	2005	2010	2014
US	7.1	7.2	5.6	5.6	4.0	5.1	9.6	6.2
Japan	2.2	2.6	2.1	3.1	4.7	4.2	5.1	3.6
Germany	2.5	6.2	4.8	8.1	7.8	11.2	7.0	5.0
OECD						6.6	8.3	7.4
Singapore (total)	3.5	4.1	1.8	1.8	2.7	3.1	2.2	2.0
Singapore (resident)					2.2	3.7	4.1	3.1	2.7

Source: OECD (2016), unemployment rate (indicator). doi: 10.1787/997c8750-en (accessed on 22 October 2016).

Summary

The FWL has been an important fiscal lever in Singapore's strategy of sustaining growth by encouraging businesses to make the best use of Singapore's limited human resources. Compared to quotas, the FWL provides more flexibility for businesses to grow and take advantage of new growth opportunities on the upturn. At the same time, the levy regulates the use of foreign labour by equalising the costs between foreign and local workers so that resident workers continue to benefit from job growth and companies feel the pressure to raise productivity to reduce the reliance on cheap foreign labour.

Meanwhile, the Singapore government continued to expand support for businesses to invest in productivity improvements and increase fiscal investments in education and vocational training for workers. With the push to develop high-value sectors to drive economic growth, the tightening of foreign workers had been limited to the lower-skill segment. The policy of welcoming foreign professionals, managers, and executives to Singapore remained largely unchanged, especially at sectors where vacancies could not be filled from the local workforce. This supported the development of a high-value economy to drive economic growth.

Chapter 15

Putting the Population to Productive Employment

In a tight labour market, workers would negotiate for higher wages. Higher wages in turn draw more people into the workforce to meet the demand for labour. But when demand for labour falls, wages do not adjust quickly back downwards. Labour prices are downward sticky. As a result, an excess supply of labour or unemployment occurs during a downturn.

Several possible reasons have been offered by economists for the downward stickiness of wages. For example, unions might have negotiated comprehensive agreements with employers that are binding for a few years. Or there may be a national minimum wage legislation that prevents employers from offering lower wages. Workers who have left jobs may also be rejecting job offers at reduced wages in expectation of better offers. Employers might also prefer to lay off less productive workers rather than reduce wages which might affect staff morale.

Whatever the reasons, the inability of wages to adjust downwards is problematic. The skills of workers who have been unemployed for long periods would deteriorate or become obsolete if wages take too long to adjust downwards to a level at which firms would be encouraged to employ the workers. It would become more difficult for these workers to get re-employed. Many would eventually give up looking for work and drop out of the labour market altogether. This would impose a cost on society. The economic potential of the nation falls, and the burden of sustaining a larger unemployed population falls on a smaller workforce. Therefore, the Singapore government has developed several tools to enhance the responsiveness of wages so that employment remains high regardless of the economic cycle.

CPF Contribution Rates

The CPF was instituted in 1955 as a fiscally prudent and sustainable tool to help workers save for retirement. The contributions by the worker and his employer under the CPF scheme would constitute the savings of the worker, which he could draw down upon retirement.

CPF contributions were initially set at just 5% of wages by each side (worker and employer). This was raised gradually to 25% from 1968 to 1985 for both the worker and the employer, totaling up to 50% of wages. From 1979 to 1984, the government also championed a high wage policy to induce the industries to raise productivity to match the high wage costs.[66] However, while the intent of the policy was to accelerate the restructuring of the economy, the resulting high costs of labour in Singapore contributed to the loss of competitiveness, which coincided with a global slowdown. This led to the city state's first recession in 1985. GDP growth rate dipped to –0.7% in 1985 and 1.3% in 1986 from 8.8% in 1984. Overall unemployment jumped from less than 3% in 1984 to 4.1% in 1985 and 6.5% in 1986.

CPF contributions effectively reduce the take-home pay of the worker and his consumption expenditures. Until the early 1980s, the government was able to "recycle" the high levels of savings back into the economy by allowing the use of CPF for purchase of public housing. But the slowdown in the growth of home ownership in the early 1980s meant that the increase in CPF savings exceeded the payments for new homes, leading to a significant extraction from the economy.

In response to the recession in 1985, the government decided to reverse its high-wage policies. It called for "wage restraint" rather than a wage cut, which would reduce the morale of the workforce. But for the first time, the total CPF contribution rate was reduced in 1985 from 50% to 35% by cutting the employer's contributions by 15% and leaving the worker's contributions untouched. Practically, workers did not consider their CPF contributions as part of their wages since they could only withdraw their CPF savings after retirement. But to employers, the CPF contributions were a significant part of wage costs. The CPF rates cut in 1985 resulted immediately in lower wage costs on the employer's side, without affecting the take-home pay for the worker. By a stroke of policy, the downward stickiness of labour costs was overcome. The lower labour costs restored export competitiveness. The economy rebounded and employment recovered.

Introduction of Flexible-Wage Policy

To overcome the rigidities in wage structure and allow individual companies to adjust to rapidly changing economic conditions, the Employment Amendment Act was enacted in 1988 to institute a "flexi-wage policy". Under the scheme, total wages would comprise an annual variable component (AVC), to be paid out annually as a lump sum above the contracted "basic" wages. Companies could cut the variable components based on economic conditions. A monthly variable component (MVC) was instituted in the early 2000s to give companies the flexibility to adjust monthly wages rather than wait till the end of the year to adjust the AVC. The implementation of the flexible-wage policy would provide an alternative way for companies to adjust wages in the absence of government-instituted CPF cuts.

After the implementation of the flexi-wage policy from 1988, the CPF cuts were slowly restored to 40% in 1991. However, the application of the flexible-wage system was uneven even though the public sector took the lead in its implementation. Subsequently, when Singapore was hit by the Asian Financial Crisis, employers' contribution rates were cut by 10 percentage points in 1999 to regain Singapore's cost competitiveness and preserve jobs. The government restored part of the cuts in 2001 as the economy recovered, but employers' contributions were again cut in 2003 when resident unemployment rose to 5.2%, the highest level since the 1985 recession.

Lower CPF Rates for Older Workers

As the population aged, the lower employment rates of older workers became an issue of concern. The government therefore lowered CPF rates for older workers (aged above 55) in 1988. Lower employer contribution rates reduced the costs of older workers to employers while the lower employee contribution rates meant larger take-home pay which encouraged more older workers to enter the labour market. Contributions for employees aged 50–55 years were cut further in 2005 to increase their employability (see Fig. 8).

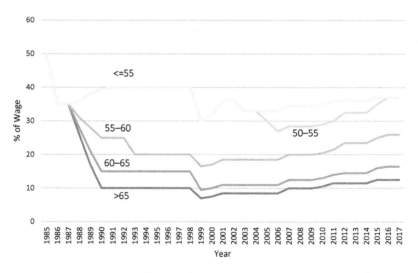

Figure 8: Total CPF Contribution Rates (Sum of Employer and Employee Contributions).

Source: Data up to 2008 has been compiled from data in "CPF Trends" (CPF, 2008); data from 2009 has been compiled by the author from various sources.

Reductions in CPF Contribution Ceiling

The CPF contribution ceiling limits the contributions that workers and employers have to make to the CPF. For example, a ceiling of $5,500 means that CPF contributions are not required for the amounts earned above $5,500 every month. The CPF contribution ceiling was reduced from $5,500 to $4,500 in two stages from 2004 to 2006 to further reduce wage costs for employees beyond the reduction in CPF contribution rates. The government subsequently brought the CPF contribution ceiling back up from S$4,500 to $5,000 in 2011 and $6,000 in 2016.

Workfare Income Supplement Scheme

From 2007, the government progressively restored the CPF cuts in view of robust job growth. It was also during this time that the government introduced the Workfare Income Supplement (WIS) scheme, which gave the government another tool to overcome the downward wage stickiness resulting from a mismatch between the worker's wage expectations and what employers are prepared to pay.

For workers who lack relevant skills, including older and displaced workers as well as the long-term unemployed such as full-time housewives returning to the workforce, employers are prepared to offer only low wages that commensurate with the lower productivity of these workers. However, many workers find the low wages too low to be worth their while going back to work. By topping up the wages offered by the employers through cash payments, WIS raises the take-home pay to match the expectations of a larger number of the lower-skill workers. The WIS also tops up their CPF contributions to boost their retirement savings as long as they continue to work.

With the implementation of WIS and nationwide efforts to enhance the employability of older workers and make flexible work arrangements available, the labour force participation rate (LFPR) of older residents aged 55 to 64 rose from 56.3% in 2006 to 69.5% in 2015. The female LFPR also rose from 54.3% to 60.4% over the same period.[67]

Shift towards Fiscal Interventions for Wage Adjustments in a Downturn

In the aftermath of the Global Financial Crisis (2008), the government chose to draw down on its past reserves in 2009 to help businesses keep local workers on the payroll through the Jobs Credit scheme. Through this scheme, businesses receive cash grants from the government based on the wage cost of the business. This temporary wage subsidy programme enabled businesses to cope with labour costs without retrenching workers, cutting wages or reducing CPF contributions. It marked the first time that the government intervened directly through fiscal injections rather than rely on CPF cuts to help businesses cope with a downturn. Jobs Credit helped keep resident unemployment to 4.3% in 2009, lower than the earlier peak of 5.2% when Singapore was hit by SARS in 2003. Unemployment fell further to 3.1% in 2010 when GDP grew 14.8% up from –0.8% in 2009.

Summary

From 1985, CPF contributions have been periodically cut during recessions or periods of low growth to enhance the employability of workers. However, cutting CPF contributions also means that the workers have less for retirement — the need to make adequate provisions for retirement is traded off for the objective of reducing labour costs to keep employment up. Furthermore, as CPF savings are also used for housing, education, and medical needs, the cuts also affected the availability of CPF funds for these purposes.

Notwithstanding the implementation of flexi-wage policy in 1988, the government continued to use CPF cuts as a way to adjust wage costs further downwards to keep employment up, especially among older and lower-skill workers till 2007, when the government implemented WIS. This allowed the government to reduce the reliance on cutting the CPF contributions of the lower-skill and older workers to improve their employability. In fact, the CPF rates of older workers above 55 have been raised several times since then. The CPF ceiling, which was brought down from $5,500 to $4,500 from 2004 to 2006, was restored to $5,000 in 2011 and $6,000 in 2016. The government also enhanced the WIS payouts several times in 2010, 2013, and 2016 to benefit more Singaporeans. During the 2009 recession, instead of cutting CPF contributions, discretionary fiscal intervention in the form of the Jobs Credit scheme was implemented to help businesses cope with keep workers employed during the downturn. The implementation of WIS and Jobs Credit marked a strategic shift from cutting CPF towards fiscal interventions to keep employment up.

SECTION IV

ADDRESSING PEOPLE'S NEEDS

Chapter 16

Jobs and Wage Growth

When Singapore became independent in 1965, average annual unemployment was 9.2%. The industrialisation programme undertaken by the government successfully attracted foreign investments which created jobs for Singaporeans. Unemployment fell consistently through two decades until Singapore's first recession in 1985, when overall unemployment rose to 4.1% in 1985 from less than 3% in the previous 4 years.

Decisive fiscal measures, including extra-budgetary measures such as the cutting of CPF contribution rates, helped reduce business costs following the 1985 recession. In the wake of tax restructuring and investments in the upgrading of workers and business capabilities, the economy moved upstream and became more competitive in higher value-add sectors. Resident unemployment[r] fell to record lows in the early 1990s at around 2%.

From 1998, unemployment crept upwards following the Asian Financial Crisis, the bursting of the tech bubble in the US, and intensification of global competition with the entry of China into the World Trade Organisation in 2001. Resident unemployment went up to more than 4% from 2002 to 2005. Nevertheless, jobs continued to be created in new economic activities, including in the services sector,

---

[r] Resident unemployment figures were not available prior to 1990.

125

that emerged in the wake of economic restructuring. Unemployment trended back to 3.0% in 2007. Although unemployment rebounded to 3.2% in 2008 and 4.3% in 2009 because of the Global Financial Crisis, it has fallen to 3% or lower since 2010 as Singapore pushed on with economic restructuring to strengthen its economic competitiveness and seek out new niches in the global economy.

Addressing Cyclical and Structural Unemployment

Against the backdrop of increasing volatility in economic growth and unemployment, a group of local economists has recently proposed the implementation of social insurance schemes to pool the risks of economic dislocation among the population, not unlike the pooling of longevity risks and risks of catastrophic medical expenditures through the CPF Life and MediShield Life schemes.[68] The argument is that some form of social insurance, such as wage loss insurance, could be designed thoughtfully to mitigate the moral hazards that have bred a culture of entitlement in the welfare states of western economies. For example, payouts could be limited to a fixed period such as 6 months and pegged to the learning of new skills and staying employed. The existence of such a scheme would reduce the resistance of displaced workers to hold out for higher paying jobs and encourage them to take up employment in different sectors as soon as possible, even at lower salaries. This would enable Singapore to push ahead with measures to restructure its economy and raise productivity levels.

The idea of unemployment insurance to provide help for vulnerable workers has also been debated in parliament from as far back as in 2006. The government decided not to have unemployment insurance because of several concerns.[69] First, if employers were to be required to make contributions to the unemployment insurance fund, the higher costs would reduce the competitiveness of export-oriented businesses and encourage the businesses to relocate or fold up. Businesses may also be induced to withdraw the payment of retrenchment benefits, which is still a widely practised norm in Singapore. Second, if the unemployment insurance contributions were to be deducted from salaries, the take-home pay of workers would fall. Alternatively, if the contributions to the insurance fund were to be taken out of their CPF contributions, retirement savings would be adversely affected. Third, unemployment insurance has an inherent moral hazard problem that could turn the scheme into benefits for the unemployed financed by the working population. If the scheme involved insuring against wage loss suffered by the re-employed worker, the payment of replacement wages would erode the incentive of the worker to upgrade or to reskill to become more productive in the new sector.

The government has thus chosen to help displaced workers through fiscal interventions instead. In a downturn, the government provides fiscal support to help viable businesses manage with costs and keep workers on the payroll. For example, the Jobs Credit scheme implemented during 2009 provided businesses with cash grants based on the payroll costs of the businesses. To address structural unemployment, schemes such as the Career Support Programme, Professional Conversion Programme, and the Place and Train Programme have been implemented and recently enhanced in Budget 2017 to better help displaced workers retrain and encourage employers to employ them at various levels. These measures are funded out of general taxation rather than as additional costs to businesses or deductions from employees' salaries. Together with other measures such as the WIS scheme, which supplements the income of low-skill workers to encourage them to stay in formal employment, these interventions allow the market to work and enable the economy to restructure and grow, while encouraging workers, especially low-skill ones, to stay employed, upgrade, retrain, and eventually to take care of themselves.

Besides encouraging individual self-reliance, the government has also been promoting social resilience by encouraging philanthropy through fiscal incentives. Charitable giving is largely encouraged through the fiscal tool of tax deductions, which benefit the higher-income groups more given the progressive income tax structures. The government also provides dollar-for-dollar matching grants for donations made to certain causes such as the self-help groups[s] and the Community Chest. By encouraging those who have done well to help those who are in need, these measures promote self-reliance at the social level.

Redistributive Impact of Fiscal Measures

The median gross monthly income in Singapore rose by six times in real terms from 1965 to 2014, after accounting for inflation. However, income growth of lower-income households has been lower than that experienced by the higher-income groups in recent years. For the lower-income Singaporean worker at the 20th percentile, the increase was about 5.5 times[t] according to an MOF estimate.[70]

As low-cost countries such as India and China opened up to the world and participated in global trade, the surplus of unskilled and low-skill labour at the global level has driven down wages at the lower end, while growing demand for professionals in growth sectors, such as finance, healthcare, and business services such as legal and consulting services, has pushed up the wages at the other end. This gap in wage growth was particularly pronounced in the 2000s as integration of economies around the world intensified.

In Singapore, incomes for the 20th percentile and median citizen worker grew a cumulative 14.8% and 21.4%, respectively, from 2004 to 2014 in real terms (after factoring the effect of inflation), with most of the growth taking place in the latter half of the decade. At the household level, the average monthly household income per member

---

[s] Chinese Development Assistance Council (CDAC), Eurasian Association (EA), and Singapore Indian Development Association (SINDA).

[t] Factory workers who made rubber slippers were paid about $87 a month in 1965 (around $340 in 2014 dollars). That was slightly less than half the average wage at the time. The lower-income Singaporean worker (at the 20th percentile of the income range) earned about $1,860 in 2014.

at the bottom and third quintiles grew more at 24.1% and 35.5%, respectively, because more members of the households entered the workforce.

MOF's computation based on the best available data shows that Singapore's Gini coefficient, measured on the per household member basis, has been above 0.40 since 1980. The Gini coefficient is a summary statistic used to measure how incomes are distributed in an economy. A Gini coefficient of zero reflects perfect equality where every household has the same income, whereas a Gini coefficient of 1 signifies an economy where one household has all the income generated. It declined from around 0.44 in 1980 to about 0.41 in 1990. Subsequently, the Gini increased in the 1990s and early 2000s to a peak of about 0.48 in 2007, which then declined to below 0.45 in 2016. Advanced economies around the world as represented by the country members of the Organisation for Economic Co-operation and Development (OECD) also experienced increasing trends in the Gini coefficient before taxes and transfers. According to MOF, these Gini coefficients are higher on average than Singapore's.

Nevertheless, Singapore's fiscal system has narrowed the income gap at the household level through a progressive tax and transfer system. The "after-taxes-and-transfers" Gini coefficient, which was computed as 0.40 for 2016, has been on a decreasing trend since 2000 even as the "before-taxes-and-transfers" Gini coefficient increased. This is attributed to the government's policies to increase the redistribution impact of fiscal measures to mitigate the widening income gap over the years.

In spite of the regressive nature of indirect taxes such as GST, a highly progressive PIT structure continues to ensure that top-tier households by income bear the bulk of all taxes. Higher-income earners pay a proportionately higher tax. Exemptions are also provided so that lower-income workers do not need to pay any tax. In 2013, property tax was made more progressive such that those who live in high-value properties and owners of investment properties pay more. After taking into account various tax reliefs and exemptions, the effective income tax rate on the median worker is close to zero. In fact, the top 10 per cent of tax payers pay over 80 per cent of PITs. If all taxes (excluding GST), fees, and charges are considered, the total effective tax rate for the average worker is only 2%.[71]

Fiscal transfers and social benefits are also provided by the government progressively. While subsidies for public services such as healthcare, housing, and education are widely available to all Singaporeans, additional subsidies are provided for lower-income households. Through the GST Voucher scheme, additional cash transfers and subsidies for utilities bills and conservancy charges are channelled to lower-income households. Since 2007, the WIS scheme has provided cash transfers to lower-wage workers who continue to stay in formal employment.

Based on an estimate by MOF in 2015,[72] the top income quintile of Singaporean households pay 55.2% of all taxes,[u] whereas the bottom quintile pay 8.5%. The lower two deciles receive 27.5% of total social benefits and transfers[v] provided by the government, whereas 11.9% are allocated to the upper two deciles. After taking into account taxes and transfers, the per person monthly household income at the bottom quintile grew the most at 45.7% over the period from 2004 to 2014. (see Fig. 9 reproduced from the 2015 MOF study).

The progressivity of the tax and transfer system is continually being enhanced. In Budget 2015, the government announced that top bracket PIT rate will be raised from 20% to 22% from the year of assessment (YA) 2017. This was followed up with the announcement in Budget 2016 that with effect from YA 2018, a cap of $80,000 will be imposed on PIT reliefs, which tended to benefit the rich, to preserve the progressivity of income tax. Transfers to the lower-income would also be enhanced. The government initiated the Silver Support scheme to provide cash transfers to poorer Singaporeans in their retirement years from 2016. The GST Voucher scheme was also

---

[u] Taxes include income tax, GST, property-related taxes, vehicle-related taxes, foreign domestic worker levies and other indirect taxes.
[v] Transfers include housing, education, health, employment, marriage and parenthood, social support, and special transfers.

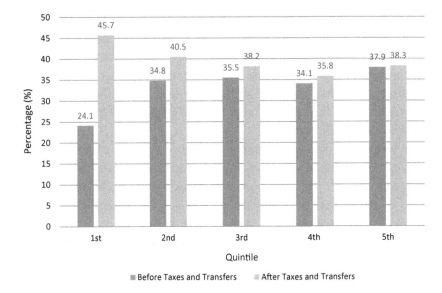

Figure 9: Cumulative Growth (%) of Real Average Monthly Household Income from Work per Member by Quintiles (2004–2014).ʷ

enhanced in Budget 2017 to help lower-income households cope with rising costs.

Boosting Wage Growth of Lower-Skill Workers

In addition to taxes and transfers, some countries around the world have also implemented a minimum wage to mitigate the increasing wage gap. The issue of minimum wage was debated in Singapore's

---

ʷ Based on ranking of citizen-employed households by monthly household income from work (including employer CPF contributions) per household member. The difference between growth rates of household incomes and growth rates of individual incomes from work over the period is due to the higher participation rate of labour among older workers and women. In other words, the income growth at the household level includes the income growth of those who are already working as well as the additional income from having more members of the households in the workforce.

parliament several times in recent years. Fundamentally, the main argument for a minimum wage policy is that it would prevent vulnerable workers from being exploited and help reduce income inequality. The minimum wage could also draw underemployed workers into the workforce and raise the LFPR. It could also be applied to foreign workers and be set at a level to create the environment to spur businesses to raise productivity.

In response, the government has reiterated that as wages are determined by the labour market at the marginal productivity of the worker employed, the minimum wage would have to be set at levels above the marginal productivity of low-wage workers for it to be effective in raising the wages of the workers. But as employers would not be prepared to pay the minimum wage for the less productive workers, it would make it more difficult for the lower-skill workers, the group which the minimum wage policy is supposed to help, to find jobs. The implementation of a minimum wage alone would also impose higher costs on businesses and reduce their international competitiveness. In an open economy like Singapore, the higher wage costs for companies would force some, especially the labour-intensive ones, to relocate to countries where labour costs are lower. SMEs who cannot afford the higher labour costs but are too small to move may eventually be forced to close down. A minimum wage would also reduce the flexibility of the labour markets to adjust wages downwards to reduce unemployment in a downturn, when more people are looking for work. The final outcome would be higher unemployment among the low-skill workforce, most of whom would be from disadvantaged backgrounds.

Instead of imposing on businesses the costs of raising the salaries of low-skill workers, the government has taken on the costs of implementing the WIS scheme in 2007. Workers benefitting from WIS are also given substantial support to upgrade their skills and become more employable through the WTS scheme. The PIC scheme was implemented in 2011 to support the efforts of businesses to improve productivity. The businesses were also encouraged to pass on productivity improvements to workers through the Wage Credit scheme

(WCS), under which the government would pay for part of the salary increases.

The government has also implemented a sectoral minimum wage through the progressive wage system (PWS) for selected sectors which are not subject to international competition and are less price sensitive, such as the cleaning and security services. To ensure that the minimum wage would not affect the employment prospects of existing low-wage workers in the sector, the PWS allows for salary ranges to be determined based on the existing productivity of the workers. In addition, the PWS provides for the workers to earn higher wages as they undergo training to improve their productivity. Under the system, the worker can move to a higher salary range when her or she becomes more skilled, based on certification offered by accredited training programmes. This provides a career path for the workers, who therefore have the incentives to undergo training, subsidised by government schemes such the WTS, to improve their skills and productivity to earn higher wages.

Though WIS, WTS, and the PWS are permanent schemes, PIC and WCS are part of a transition support package to help businesses adjust to rising costs as they restructure, which would be phased out in stages from 2016 to 2018. Nevertheless, the government has announced in Budget 2015 new programmes under the SkillsFuture initiative which would provide substantial fiscal support to help workers develop industry-relevant skills to stay employed and earn higher wages. The fundamental approach taken by the government therefore is to help workers stay employable and enable them to earn higher salaries by improving their skills and productivity rather than simply legislating higher wages, which on its own would lead to higher unemployment, especially among low-skill workers.

Chapter 17

Ensuring Visible Broad-Based Benefits

Larger countries such as the United States have the scale in land, vibrancy of workforce, and depth of capital that provide for redundancy in capacity and diversity in skills and technology to support the creation of new capabilities to serve new needs and even shape the market. But for a small nation with little natural resources, the Singapore government has to plan long term and intervene rigorously in the markets to mobilise the limited resources of land and labour to support national economic strategies for growth.

Singapore has to continually reinvent itself to stay relevant in a global landscape where change is accelerating. The Singapore government has been taking the lead to develop master plans for economic restructuring by regularly reviewing geopolitical, economic, and technological trends that are expected to drive global changes over the long term. These plans serve to coordinate the efforts of various stakeholders — the government, businesses, unions, universities, and workers — in the restructuring of the economy to promptly take advantage of opportunities as they emerge.

The availability of substantial fiscal resources accumulated over time through prudent fiscal policies has served to instill confidence in the small island state's ability to sustain large investments over the long term for the development of new capabilities to support economic growth. But the government needs to earn the support of the people to implement the economic master plans, which usually span over several electoral cycles. Fiscal strategies must therefore also continually yield tangible and broad-based benefits to the people. While fiscal resources are being set aside for future needs, the current needs of Singaporeans cannot be ignored.

When Singapore became independent, besides job creation, the government also set out to address the needs of the Singapore population in the areas of national security, housing, education, and health, which were assessed to be the top priorities in that order.[73]

National Security

Singapore is not only a city but also a sovereign nation. Besides addressing the social needs of the population, the Singapore government invests heavily in national defence and internal security. After the British indicated that it would withdraw its troops from Singapore in 1971, the government announced a plan to increase defence expenditure to 10% of gross national product (GNP).[74] Defence spending, which has since then trended down to about 4–5% of GDP in the 2000s and about 3% since 2010, has always been the largest item in the annual budget. The investments in defence capabilities have preserved the peace, progress, and prosperity that the city state has worked hard to create since its independence.

The large defence expenditures are also generally seen by citizens as not only necessary for a small nation surrounded by large neighbours but also useful for nation building. The Singapore military system relies on a large pool of conscripts in the active and reserve armed forces. Singapore male youths are brought together in a collective life when they are conscripted to undertake national service in the army. Thereafter, they could be recalled to undergo reservist training until the statutory age of 50 years (for senior ranks) and 40 years (for other ranks). The reservists or national servicemen make up around four fifths of the Singapore Armed Forces (SAF). The SAF has been a national pride for the people of Singapore. The contributions by SAF to the rescue and recovery efforts in neighbouring countries when they are affected by natural disasters have received broad-based support from the people.

By comparison, expenditures on internal security are much smaller at around 1% of GDP. But due to a combination of strong legislation against crime and investments in enforcement capabilities, Singapore has one of the lowest crime rates in the world. This has not always been the case. Serious and organised crimes such as armed robbery, kidnapping, and drug trafficking, which were not uncommon in the earlier days of newly independent Singapore, have fallen significantly over the years because of the firm and decisive action taken by the Singapore government against crime. Singaporeans now enjoy safety and security, and this has contributed to a liveable environment conducive for work and play.

Homes for All

The most visible area of progress made since Singapore's independence has been in housing. After Singapore was granted self-government in 1959, one of the major initiatives that the government embarked on was to meet the pressing need for low-cost housing. A large percentage of the population, an estimated 550,000, were living either in squatter settlements without access to sanitation or water or in overcrowded shophouses in the town area.[75]

HDB was established in 1960 to solve the housing problem. By 1963, HDB had built 31,317 flats and successfully tackled the housing crisis. The flats were basic, but they provided decent housing and shelter with piped water and clean sanitation. HDB flats were first available for rental only and it was only in 1964 that HDB units became available for sale on 99-year leases, under a "Home Ownership for the People" scheme. They were sold to households with incomes not exceeding $800 a month. Singaporean households were offered loans so that they paid less in monthly mortgage payments than they would have done in rents.[76] In addition, the rules were relaxed to allow Singaporeans to make use of their savings in the CPF to pay for the HDB homes, thereby reducing the cash outlays for the mortgage repayments.

By 1990, more than eight in ten Singaporeans were living in HDB flats with more than 90% owning their flats. Beyond just the low price, the HDB flats were built within comprehensively planned self-contained towns with community facilities such as schools, community centres, and parks, and services such as wet markets, hawker centres, and convenience stores, that served the needs of residents. In the earlier phases, light industrial estates built by JTC were located near to the HDB towns so that the residents could also find employment nearby. Estate management such as cleaning of common areas, lift maintenance, and the provision of parking and other services such as waste disposal were also ably handled initially by HDB and later by town councils. A diversity of flat sizes and designs were built to meet the various needs of the population. The comprehensive approach to the development of HDB estates brought visible improvements in living conditions, and the Home Ownership scheme was an overwhelming success.

The focus of HDB had been on churning out as many flats as possible in the 1960s and 1970s. From the 1980s, HDB began to focus on building flats of a higher quality. Between 1990 and 2012, the government embarked on a Main Upgrading Programme to enhance the overall living environment of older HDB flats, including retrofitting the interior fittings of flats. The programme benefited more than 130,000 households and costed the government around $3.3 billion.[77] A Home Improvement Programme was announced in 2007 to upgrade HDB flats which were built until 1986 and had not undergone the Main Upgrading Programme. Another 300,000 HDB flats were expected to benefit from the programme.[78]

Over time, with the growth in incomes, and upgrading of HDB facilities, home owners have enjoyed appreciation in the values of their HDB properties. The HDB estates, which have been designed to encourage community interaction, also promoted social cohesion across Singaporeans from various backgrounds, income levels, and ethnic groups. Therefore, the government provides grants for Singaporeans up to a household income of $12,000 to encourage Singaporeans to live in HDB estates. Additional housing grants are provided on a means-tested basis to lower and middle-income households earning up to $8,000 per month[x] to ensure affordability of HDB flats to all. To meet the aspirations of younger middle-income households to own private properties, the government also introduced the Executive Condominium scheme in 1996, which allows private developers to develop condominium estates to be sold to higher-income Singaporean households. Households earning up to $14,000 per month, who qualify to purchase the executive condominiums, also enjoy housing grants under the scheme.

A minimum occupation period is imposed on both the HDB flats and executive condominiums before the Singaporean owners can sell them on the secondary markets. Permanent residents can purchase resale HDB flats and executive condominiums in the secondary markets. After a certain specified period, the executive condominiums will be privatised and the owners of these properties can sell them to foreign buyers as well. The HDB flats and executive condominiums have therefore also become assets which can be monetised, although rules are in place to make sure that they remain primarily for owner-occupation.

As the population ages, the government began building studio apartments to meet the needs of an increasing number of elderly households who were looking to relocate from their larger flats after their children moved out to their own homes. A Silver Housing Bonus scheme was put in place to provide additional help for ageing households to downsize and move to smaller, cheaper homes. If the elderly wished to age in the familiarity of their own homes and neighbourhood, they could also "sell" the tail end of the leases of the flats which they had been staying in back to the government through a Lease Buyback scheme. These schemes help the elderly monetise the value of the HDB flats to supplement their retirement incomes.

---

[x] Median monthly household income from work in 2015 was $8,666.

The total costs of the subsidies paid out of the budget for the Housing Programme varied year to year because of changes to the costs of construction and land, as well as the sales price of the HDB flat and the volume of sales (which varied according to the property cycle). For the financial year ended 31 March 2016, the government provided a grant of $1.6 billion to subsidise the sale of HDB flats, almost a quarter less than the $2.2 billion in subsidies provided the year before.[79] Although the costs of the Silver Housing Bonus scheme and the Lease Buyback scheme are still a small part of the housing costs, these would grow in significance as the population ages and take-up rates increase when households become more familiar with the schemes.

Education

In the initial years, the focus of government spending on education was on providing universal education. This led to a period of rapid construction of 83 new school buildings from 1959 to 1965 — about one new school every month. By 1970, there were no more shortages of primary schools and secondary schools.[80] Primary school enrolment rose by more than 100,000 from 272,000 in 1959 to peak in 1968 at 380,000 after which enrolment fell due to falling cohort sizes. Secondary enrolment increases were more impressive, more than tripling from 49,000 in 1959 to 176,000 in 1975.[81] The government also began investing in technical education in 1968 to equip students with practical skills that enhanced their employability on entering the workforce.[82] When the initial quantitative demands for education in terms of enrolment numbers had been met, the government shifted its focus in the 1980s to raising quality and started to invest into diversifying the educational system to cater to the different learning needs of students to optimise learning outcomes.

Government spending on education as a percentage of GDP doubled from 2.7% in 1960 to 5.4% in 1970.[83] This has moderated to around 3% of GDP currently. Although this is low in comparison with other advanced countries such as the UK or US which spend in excess of 5% of GDP, Singapore's education spending as a share of the government's total budget is larger at around 20%.[84] In fact, government recurrent spending per student at various levels from primary schools to junior colleges, institutes of technical education and polytechnics has risen steadily in real terms over the last three decades from 1986 to 2015 (see Fig. 10). Government recurrent spending per student at universities has roughly kept pace with inflation even as the cohort participation rate for publicly funded universities has risen over the same period.

Education at the primary and secondary levels is now virtually free. Although the government provides a subsidy that covers the bulk of the operating and infrastructural costs for post-secondary education institutes such as the institutes of technical education, polytechnics, and universities, the students at these institutions pay fees pegged at a percentage of the costs (up to around one fifth to one quarter of the total costs for universities) to reflect that

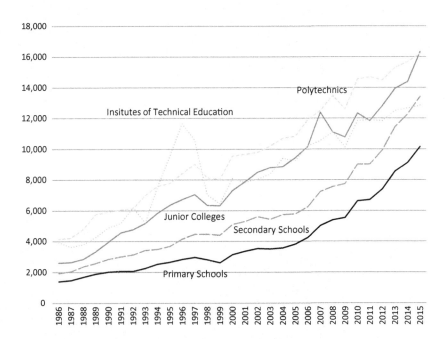

Figure 10: Annual Government Recurrent Expenditure on Education per Student.
Source: Data generated by SingStat Table Builder (12 December 2016).

significant benefits of higher education accrue to the student in terms of increased employability and expected earnings from the education expenditure. Besides spurring the students to make the best use of the learning opportunities so that they graduate within the expected candidature periods, the post-secondary education institutes would also be accountable to the students in terms of making sure that the courses offered are relevant and would enable the students to move on to good jobs on graduation. The Singapore government provides financial assistance, as well as subsidised loans and bursaries, to help students from lower-income homes with the course fees so that no one would be denied an education just because they cannot afford it.

In terms of education outcomes, Singapore's education system has been hailed internationally as one of the world's best. Virtually every child in each cohort goes through the primary and secondary education now. Singapore students consistently achieve high Programme for International Student Assessment (PISA) scores. Post-secondary education is predominantly skills based, providing vocational training to around 70% of each cohort through well-funded institutes of technical education and polytechnics. In 2015, around 30% of each cohort went through government-funded universities,[y] and the government is planning to raise the figure to 40% by 2020. The government also plans to provide support for 10% of each cohort to pursue continuing education and training (CET) degrees by 2020. These investments serve to enhance the capabilities of the Singaporean workforce and give Singaporeans the confidence and ability to thrive as knowledge workers in an increasingly competitive global economy. The World Economic Forum's Global Competitive Report 2016 ranked Singapore second in terms of the "Quality of Education System" and the International Institute for Management Development's *World Competitiveness Yearbook 2016* ranked Singapore third and joint second, respectively, in the categories "Education System Meets Needs of a Competitive Economy" and "University Education".

---

[y] Including graduates from polytechnics and institutes of technical education.

Healthcare

Though healthcare was not a top priority to which limited fiscal resources were allocated in the early years of nation building, Singapore invested wisely in the low-lying fruits of public health initiatives, such as vaccination, environmental regulation regarding sanitation, clean food and water, and control of infectious diseases, which yielded remarkable results. A network of satellite outpatient dispensaries and clinics, which were developed at relatively low costs, also proved to be effective in bringing basic primary care services to the people and took the pressure off the hospitals.[85]

Healthcare services had been free under the British system. When the Singapore government took over, it imposed a fee of 50 cents[86] for visits to public clinics as a reminder that public services came at a cost. The user co-payment principle has since then been a key plank of Singapore's fiscal strategies to inculcate self-reliance among Singaporeans and curb wasteful usage of public services. This has also been instrumental in keeping Singapore's healthcare spending on a sustainable trend.

The CPF scheme, which was first instituted to help workers save for retirement, was also expanded to include saving for medical expenses. A proportion of the worker's CPF contributions is allocated to a MediSave account, which could be used to offset large expenses in the hospitals or specific outpatient medical services. The user co-payment policy is intended to reinforce the message that healthcare is a personal responsibility and to encourage Singaporeans to avoid large medical expenses through healthy living habits.

Nevertheless, the demand for healthcare is projected to grow, driven by an ageing population. The old-age support ratio[z] has declined by two-thirds from around 21 in 1965 to around 7 in 2014, with almost half of the decline taking place in the last 20 years. The Singapore government has been making investments to increase the capacities in medical infrastructure, such as by building new hospitals, polyclinics, step-down care facilities, and nursing homes. Medical

---

[z] The ratio of population aged 15–64 to population aged 65 and older.

advances which made more medical conditions treatable have also raised the costs of medical care. Government spending on healthcare has therefore been on an upward trend. In 2006, total government spending on healthcare was $1.9 billion or about 1% of GDP. This grew by more than five times to $10.7 billion in 2017 or 2.5% of GDP (budgeted) and is expected to continue growing (see Fig. 11).

The Singapore government relies on a combination of market forces and intervention to keep medical costs low. First, the government is the main supplier of healthcare, especially acute care through a network of hospitals and polyclinics operated by national healthcare providers owned by the government. Although the national healthcare providers are run like private operators with autonomy in management and recruitment and responsibility of maintaining financial sustainability, they are not for profit, and their mandate is to ensure that a range of medical services are available to the public at reasonable costs.

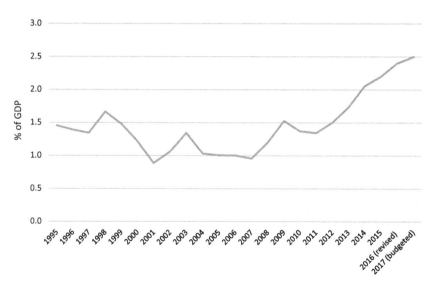

Figure 11: Government Expenditure (% of GDP) on Healthcare (1995–2016).

Source: 1995–2014: The World Bank Databank, accessed 14 October 2016; 2015–2017: Analysis of Revenue and Expenditure Financial Year 2017 (Ministry of Finance, 20 February 2017).

Having more than one national healthcare provider has enabled the government to lower costs through competition. The government also provides subsidies to patients through the healthcare providers for a package of medical services that has been assessed to be cost-effective and beneficial for the population in general. In line with the principle of co-payment to promote self-reliance, patients are required to pay a share of the medical costs through fees, which helped curb wasteful and unnecessary demand for health services. Additional means-tested subsidies are also provided to lower-income patients. Beyond the basic package, the government-owned healthcare providers also offer medical treatments as well as wards with better facilities as demanded but without subsidies. Thus, patients would have the choice to proceed with unsubsidised advanced treatments if they could afford it.

To ensure large medical bills remain affordable for all, the government introduced a national medical insurance scheme (MediShield Life) to pool risks for large medical expenditures at hospitals and selected costly outpatient treatments such as dialysis and chemotherapy for cancer. The scheme is fully self-funded by premiums which are sized to provide coverage for subsidised treatments and could be paid for from CPF MediSave accounts. The premiums for lower-income households are made more affordable with government subsidies. On the other hand, those who are able to afford them could top up the national MediShield premiums to enjoy higher insurance coverage, including for non-subsidised treatments and wards.

MediShield insurance payouts are structured so that patients would still be required to make out-of-pocket payments for the medical treatments after the insurance payouts. This was designed to keep a cap on costs, which would have the tendency to escalate given that the healthcare providers would have the incentives to overprovide and the patient to overconsume. Through the MediFund, an endowment fund created by the government over time with budget surpluses, a social safety net is put in place to make sure that medical care is still accessible to those who cannot afford to pay the fees even after subsidies and insurance payouts.

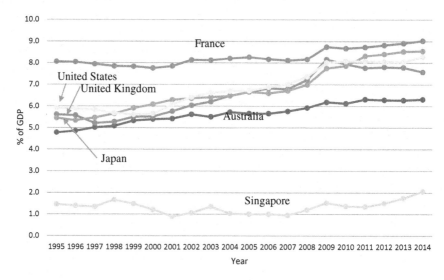

Figure 12:   Public Health Expenditure (% of GDP) from 1995 to 2014.
Source: The World Bank Databank, accessed 14 October 2016.

The healthcare system in Singapore has enabled the government to spend less on healthcare as a percentage of GDP than many advanced countries, such as the US, UK, and Japan (see Fig. 12). Notwithstanding the lower spending, Singapore is ranked sixth, ahead of Japan, the United Kingdom, and United States, in a study of the overall performance of health systems in 191 countries by the World Health Organisation in 2000.[87] France was the top-ranked country in the study, but its public expenditure was many times more than Singapore's.

Meeting Higher Order Needs

Over the years, as the basic needs were addressed and more resources became available from economic growth, the government began to commit more fiscal resources to the creation of a vibrant, liveable, and sustainable city state.

Singapore had been known as the Garden City, and more recently a City in a Garden. Soon after Singapore gained independence, a specialist Parks and Trees Unit was set up within the Public Works Department (PWD) in 1967 to ensure that provisions for trees and parks were built into the development of public works and infrastructure and coordinate the activities of the various government agencies for greening the whole island. The Parks and Trees Unit merged with the Botanic Gardens to form the Parks and Recreation Department in 1975. In 1996, the department became instituted as the National Parks Board, a statutory board which in addition to being responsible for the maintenance of parks and roadside greenery was also charged with the development of new parks and upgrading of existing ones. As the island has become more urbanised over the years, the fiscal resources provided to National Parks have grown in tandem with the intensification of greening efforts to soften the concrete landscape by creating a garden environment that is enjoyed by all Singaporeans. From the 2000s, National Parks embarked on the development of a comprehensive network of park connectors to link parks and green spaces for better access and enjoyment by the community. National Parks also began building up the capabilities to conserve the rich biodiversity of the island city state. The operating budget allocated to National Parks grew from around $101 million in 2005 to $311 million (budgeted) in 2017.[88] Substantial developmental expenditures were also incurred for projects, for example, more than $1 billion for the Gardens by the Bay which opened to the public in 2012.

A large part of building a liveable city involves making Singapore a car-light society. Substantial investments are being made in this area. A $36 billion 5-year plan was announced in 2015 to expand the Mass Rapid Transport (MRT) rail network and improve the reliability of MRT services in Singapore.[89] This includes building more train stations and development of facilities such as dedicated paths for cycling and walking in the areas around the station to encourage more people to use public transport as the preferred way to get around.

The government also invested more in the development of the arts. Development of the Esplanade theatre began in 1996 to create a performing arts centre located in the middle of town. The Esplanade, which took 14 years to be completed and costed around $600 million, met the supply gap for a theatre that could host large-scale art performances. The National Arts Council (NAC) and the National Heritage Board (NHB) were set up in the early 1990s to promote the development of the arts as well as the museum and heritage landscapes. The combined operation of these two agencies grew from $80 million in 2005 to $242 million (budgeted) in 2017.[90] Substantial development expenditures were also made to develop museums in restored historical monuments, such as the National Gallery Singapore, housed in the former City Hall and Supreme Court Building, which was retrofitted at the cost of more than $500 million.

Summary

Since independence, the judicious application of fiscal resources has yielded remarkable results that improved the lives of generations of Singaporeans. In addition to addressing the needs of the Singapore population, the investment of fiscal resources to raise the standards of living has also transformed Singapore into a vibrant global city that is attractive to investors as well as talents from around the world. This has enabled the Singapore government to earn the trust of the people to continue with its policies to sustain the growth needed to further improve the livelihoods of Singaporeans.

Chapter 18

Sharing of Surpluses

When the economy was growing strongly in the 1990s and Singapore started to have what appeared then to be structural budget surpluses, it would have been tempting for the government to engage in populist measures to either increase subsidies for public services or make social transfers more pervasive. But the Singapore government had been disciplined in keeping to the principle of budgetary prudence. "Surplus sharing" exercises were introduced to distribute the fruits of economic growth to the people in a sustainable way. These schemes were designed to be one-off and thus did not compromise on long-term budgetary sustainability and flexibility.

The surplus sharing schemes first took the form of top-ups to CPF accounts to build up the assets of Singaporeans and supplement retirement savings. The first such top-up to CPF accounts was made in 1993. In tandem with the privatisation of Singapore Telecom (SingTel) and the offer of discounted SingTel shares to CPF members, the government made transfers to CPF accounts, which recipients could use to buy stocks in blue-chip Singapore companies. The scheme was termed the CPF Share Ownership Top-Up Scheme (SOTUS), and two more SOTUS schemes were rolled out in 1995 and 1996, in conjunction with a second offering of discounted SingTel shares in 1996. After 1996, surplus sharing schemes took the form of direct top-ups to the CPF accounts, in particular, to MediSave accounts to provide for the medical needs of Singaporeans. Since then, CPF top-ups have become a regular feature of budget surplus sharing exercises.

By definition, the surplus sharing schemes are universal and broad-based so that every citizen could see the tangible benefits of growth. The benefits are also structured so that lower-income households would receive more to serve a redistribution objective. However, although CPF top-ups were generally progressive in nature, those who were not working and did not have CPF accounts did not receive any top-ups. Thus, families with no children benefitted disproportionately more than households with child dependants on the per household member basis. To address this unevenness, the government introduced the Post-Secondary Education Account (PSEA) in 2007 into which surpluses were deposited for use by younger Singaporeans who have not entered the workforce and thus do not have CPF accounts. The funds could be used for post-secondary education institutions or selected workforce training programmes, as part of an increasing emphasis on Continuous Education and Training. In 2011, the government created the Child Development Credits (CDC) scheme to make special transfers to Singaporean children aged six and below to help families with young children meet their expenses. The PSEA and the CDC schemes complement the EduSave accounts of primary and secondary school level citizens which receive annual top-ups from the EduSave fund, which is also topped-up whenever the government can afford to do so.

The other commonly used method to distribute surpluses is by way of rebates to offset fees and charges paid for by HDB flat dwellers, such as rebates for service and conservancy (S&C) charges, and utilities charges. Since 1992, the government has made transfers by way of such rebates to a broad base of Singaporeans who live in HDB flats and targeted the surplus transfers efficiently to lower-income households by incomes as well as house types so that those with lower incomes and who live in smaller flats receive more rebates. The rebates on utilities, which were later termed "U-Save" rebates, were also thoughtfully designed to be given out only in some months so that consumers would still bear the full burden of their bills in most months and not inadvertently adjust their lifestyles to consume more.

From 2001, the government began to make cash transfers in surplus sharing schemes in addition to CPF top-ups and rebates. Initially, the cash transfers were designed to incentivise savings and work. For example, the cashable shares "New Singapore Shares" ($3 billion) distributed in 2001 to help Singaporeans tide through the economic downturn following the bursting of the dot.com bubble in the United States were designed to mimic bonds such that dividends tied to economic growth would be paid yearly if people held on to their shares. The 2006 "Progress Package" included a Workfare Bonus, which is in essence a cash payout to older low-wage Singaporeans that is tied to work, that is, the person must have worked for 6 months in 2006 to be eligible for the payout.

Subsequently, cash payouts were also made to help Singaporeans cope with the painful impact of economic restructuring or to share the benefits of growth when the government has the budget surpluses to do so, for example, the issuances of cashable "Economic Restructuring Shares" of $3.6 billion from 2002 to 2004 to help Singaporeans cope with the increase in GST from 3% to 5% between 2003 and 2004. More than $2 billion in cash transfers in the form of GST credits were given from 2007 to 2010[91] to help offset the impact of GST when it was raised from 5% to 7% in 2007. This was supplemented by $870 million in "Growth Dividends" in 2008, following a year of good growth in 2007.

Businesses also received cash transfers to help cope with the restructuring of the economy, especially after the Global Financial Crisis in 2008 and 2009. In Budget 2010, the government introduced the Productivity and Innovation Credit (PIC) scheme which gave businesses 400% tax deductions on up to $400,000 of spending in qualifying activities[aa] from 2011 to 2015. Businesses have the option to convert up to $100,000 of the qualifying spending into cash grants at a specified conversion rate of up to 60%. The PIC scheme was subsequently extended to 2018 in 2014. Budget 2012

[aa] Includes training of employees, R&D, investment in design projections acquisition and licensing of intellectual property rights, and acquisition and leasing of information technology and automation equipment.

included a SME cash grant of $300 million to help SMEs cope with rising costs while the economic environment remained challenging. In Budget 2013, the government announced a significant 3-year Transition Support Package to help businesses restructure and cope with a tight labour market as the government continues to raise FWL to tighten the flow of foreign labour. The package included a PIC bonus (enhancements to the PIC scheme) and a Wage Credit scheme (WCS) under which the government would co-fund 40% of wage increases for Singaporean employees earning less than $4,000 in monthly salary between 2013 and 2015. In 2015, the PIC bonus and WCS were extended to 2017 but at reduced levels.

Over the years, surplus sharing schemes in the various forms of CPF top-ups, fee rebates, and cash transfers have become expected, especially at the end of each term of government, when the government would be expected to have chalked up some surpluses. In 2006, surplus sharing via the "Progress Package" was undertaken on the back of a modest budget surplus that followed many years of zero or negative budget balances to share with Singaporeans the "fruits of the nation's progress".[92] In 2011, a $3.2 billion "Grow and Share" package was announced to share "our surplus and provide benefits to Singaporeans",[93] while in 2015 a slew of special transfers to households and businesses totalling $5.7 billion was included in the budget.

A number of surplus sharing schemes, which have proven effective in addressing enduring underlying needs, have also been made permanent. For example, the one-off Workfare Bonus scheme in 2006 was converted to a permanent WIS scheme in 2007. The recycling back of GST increases by way of MediSave top ups, cash transfers, and utility rebates has been made permanent for lower-income households in the form of the permanent GST Voucher scheme which was introduced in Budget 2012.

Nevertheless, the government has been careful to manage any expectations for more surplus sharing schemes to be made on a regular basis. Such surplus sharing schemes are presented as "special" transfers separately from the ongoing operating and development spending of ministries to highlight that that these items are one-off and not to be expected as regular features. By taking this approach, Singapore has been able to maintain the fiscal flexibility to address the changing ephemeral needs of the people without committing to increased spending over the longer term.

SECTION V

CHALLENGES AND ISSUES FOR THE FUTURE

Chapter 19

Ageing Population

Singapore's prudent fiscal policies have worked well on the back of good demographics since independence. Its young population was willing to work hard, contribute to the economy and adapt to the restructuring that the government undertook in response to global shocks, especially over the last two decades. However, this model is increasingly coming under pressure as the population ages. In spite of various fiscal incentives provided by the government to encourage Singaporeans to have children, the resident total fertility rate has been at sub-replacement levels since the late 1970s. According to the United Nation's World Population Prospects, the ratio of those aged 65 and above to those aged 15–64 in Singapore is expected to more than double between 2010 and 2040. Such a population will be less vibrant and less able to provide for itself. Even if the elderly Singaporean undertook personal responsibility for his own health, he would be expected to consume more medical services as he ages.

The government enhanced the CPF system in 2008 to pay an additional one percent per annum on the first $60,000 combined savings of each CPF member. With effect from 2016, an additional 1 percent is paid on the first $30,000 savings of CPF members aged 55 and above. In addition, MediShield Life, implemented from 2015, provides enhanced coverage for large healthcare bills for life. These measures go some way towards helping to pay for the medical expenses of an elderly Singaporean, but he or she would still be expected to incur out-of-pocket medical expenses.

While Singapore's CPF system was intended to be a main source of retirement income for the aged, a 2010 World Bank and OECD study estimated the gross replacement rate of CPF-related payouts to be at less than 17 percent of pre-retirement wages.[94] There are no statistics on family transfers, but anecdotes suggest that elderly Singaporeans rely considerably on their working-age children and relatives for financial support. As the ratio of working age to elderly persons declines, such a family-based system of support will come under increasing pressure.

To provide more support to families that are caring for elderly parents, the government has made discretionary contributions to CPF accounts of Singaporeans from budget surpluses since the 1990s. But this has not been enough to address the needs sufficiently. The government has thus taken further steps to provide for the living expenses of the elderly. Schemes such as the Silver Housing Bonus scheme and the Lease Buyback scheme were introduced to help elderly households unlock the value of the savings invested in their HDB properties. In 2014, the government announced the Silver Support scheme which provides the bottom 20% of Singaporeans aged 65 and above with cash payouts of between $300 and $750 on a quarterly basis to supplement their retirement incomes. Currently, the scheme which covers about 30% of the senior cohorts, or 150,000 elderly persons, is expected to cost $350 million per year.[95] As the population ages, there will be more pressure for the government to enlarge the schemes and increase payouts.

The higher expected outlays for an ageing population will have to be borne by the working population. In addition, the local workforce is expected to shrink from 2020 onwards[96] as the number of young Singaporeans entering the workforce would be fewer than workers retiring. To delay the decline in the resident labour force, the government has been targeting to raise the workforce participation rates among the elderly through various schemes to expand employment opportunities for older workers, enhance the cost competitiveness of

older workers, raise their skills and value, and shape positive percep-
tions towards older workers.[97] To this end, the government has, over
more than two decades, gradually raised the retirement age from 55
to 62 to protect workers against being asked to retire before the stipu-
lated age, and requires employers to offer re-employment after age 62
until 67 or provide a payment to help the worker tide over the period
a time while he seeks alternative employment. A Special Employment
Credit is granted to employers who voluntarily re-employ workers
aged 55 and above and earning up to $4000, from 2011 to 2019.
These schemes are in addition to the WIS payouts which top up the
salaries of older low-wage workers.

While the measures have achieved some success in raising the
LFPR of older workers, it would however be increasingly difficult for
the elderly to learn the new skills required by an economy that is
restructuring at a quicker pace. His earning capacity, even if he
wanted to continue working, would fall in tandem with the deteriora-
tion of his productivity, especially as his skills lose relevance. Higher
government expenditures would be needed to train and retrain older
workers and subsidise their wages to make it worthwhile for the older
and less productive workers to stay in the workforce and encourage
employers to re-employ retired workers.

The higher expenditures to meet the needs of an ageing population must be addressed by growing the economy. Otherwise, the
public spending in various social, economic, and security needs cannot be sustained. For Singapore's economy to remain vibrant and
continue creating opportunities for its people, its ageing workforce
needs to be augmented by foreigners. In addition to the increased
spending on healthcare and employment subsidies as the population
ages, the government is also investing heavily in the development of
infrastructure so that the city state can continue to sustain a flow of
immigration for the development of a higher value economy. This
means bigger expenditures for new infrastructure, including housing
estates, roads and Mass Rapid Transit (MRT) networks, and other
community facilities such as parks. The increased developmental
expenditures are expected to bring about broad-based benefits to

Singaporeans and also pay back over time in terms of higher economic growth. But there is a limit to how much the population can grow. The growth in foreign workforce must be moderated by raising productivity so that fewer, albeit more qualified, foreign workers would be needed to sustain economic growth. Developmental spending for additional infrastructures to accommodate the workforce growth can consequently be economised and social disamenities managed. As the small city state runs up against the constraints of limited land space and a small population, its productivity movement has never been more crucial to its continued success. It is therefore imperative that the government continue to push on with and intensify its efforts to restructure the economy, such as by raising the FWL and providing fiscal support to raise productivity at the national, industry, and company levels.

Chapter 20

Headwinds in an Increasingly Turbulent World

Singapore's rise over the last half a century has been supported by benign global conditions that supported worldwide economic growth. There were no major geopolitical upheavals since the World War II ended in 1945. Although civil wars and armed conflicts had broken out in some localised regions, these were contained to their respective parts of the world. The peaceful global environment supported trade growth while technological advancements spawned new products and services that fuelled consumption growth, first in the Western World and then in emerging countries. Global trade and technological innovations have enabled markets to produce a vast range of goods and services at higher quality and lower prices. The economic growth and widespread development brought about by globalisation have lifted hundreds of millions in developing countries, such as China, India, and even Sub-Saharan Africa, out of poverty.[98]

However, while global trade has narrowed the gap between rich and poor countries, income gaps within countries have widened. FDIs have brought employment to many developing countries where the cost of labour is low, but lower-skill workers in many developed countries have lost their jobs as a consequence. On the other hand, high-skill workers, such as professionals, managers, executives, and technicians (PMETs), who are in short supply, have enjoyed wage increases especially in growth sectors such as info-communication technology, finance, and healthcare. Consequently, income inequality has grown, especially in liveable cities of the developed world, where high-skill workers from around the world congregate to tap on the economic opportunities arising from the concentration of capital, talent, and ideas. According to studies posted by the Economic Policy Institute, only the top 5% households by income levels in the US have experienced real income growth during the period 2007–2015.[99] Wage inequality has risen from the late 1970s and continued to 2015. Hourly pay for the vast majority of American workers has stagnated despite growing economy-wide productivity, with economic gains highly concentrated at the top.[100]

Many developed countries have recently begun to experience a push back from their peoples on globalisation. On 8 November 2016, Mr Donald Trump was elected as the president of the United States, the largest economy in the world. Mr Trump had pledged during his election campaign to pull out of trade agreements and implement protectionist policies to get American companies to bring back manufacturing activities that had been offshored. Businesses began changing their investment plans even before Mr Trump's swearing-in as president on 20 January 2017. On 3 January 2017, Ford Motors announced the scrapping of its plans to build a US$1.6 billion car factory in Mexico and instead invest US$700 million to expand the facilities in its Michigan factory. This announcement came almost immediately after Mr Trump criticised General Motors for manufacturing a make of Chevrolet cars in Mexico that would be shipped tax-free into the US. Mr Trump also hinted at the imposition of border taxes for goods imported into the US[101] for domestic consumption. During Mr Trump's swearing-in as the new US president, he said in his inauguration speech that "we [the US] must protect our borders from the ravages of other countries making our products, stealing our companies, and destroying our jobs. Protection will lead to great prosperity and strength." He affirmed that his administration will follow "two simple rules: Buy American and hire American." It is still not clear at this early stage of the Trump presidency how the protectionist rhetoric will translate to policies, but observers have raised the possibility of trade wars if America were to start implementing protectionist measures against countries that are exporting to the US.

However, the Trans-Pacific Partnership (TPP), which is a trade agreement among twelve of the Pacific Rim countries including Japan, Mexico, Australia, Malaysia, and Singapore, is already a casualty of free trade even at this early phase of the Trump presidency. The TPP, which would account for 40% of world trade, contained new and updated rules for cross-border trade and investment covering electronically transmitted products and protection of intellectual property rights. The agreement was signed on 4 February 2016 after 7 years of negotiations but needed to be ratified by at least six of the countries involved, who accounted for at least 85% of the total GDP of the twelve countries, before the deal entered into force. One of the first tasks that President Trump undertook after his inauguration was to issue an executive order to formally signify that the US would not be ratifying the TPP. Without ratification by the US, which accounted for the bulk of the GDP of the signatories of the TPP, there would be no other way for the agreement to be implemented in its current form. As the US is the largest economy in the world, its implementation of protectionist policies will impact world trade, disrupt global supply chains, and ultimately affect trade-dependent Singapore.

Europe is also similarly experiencing a wave of populist far-right movement. In Europe, the United Kingdom voted in a referendum held in June 2016 to leave the European Union (EU) — which has been coined as "Brexit". Analysts have offered many suggestions for the outcome of the vote, ranging from the stagnation of incomes of lower-wage workers to nationalism and frustration with the red tape of the EU. But discomfort with the inability to control the inflow of immigrants from other parts of the EU, who were seen to have taken away places in schools and jobs, played most in the minds of voters during the referendum.[102] Fundamentally, the majority of British failed to see the benefits of being in the EU. Brexit has led to concerns over the rise of "Euroscepticism" in other EU member countries who could follow in the UK's path to leave the EU. Mrs Marine Le Pen, leader of far-right National Front Party in France, called for a similar referendum in France after the UK voted to leave the EU. In the first round of the French presidential elections that took place on 24 April 2017, Mrs Le Pen emerged second out of the eleven candidates who took part in the election. The run-off round of the elections which took place on 7 May 2017 pitted Mrs Le Pen against the independent candidate Mr Emmanuel Macron, an advocate for open and free trade, and supporter of the EU, who was eventually elected as the French president. Though the election of Mr Macron has effectively pre-empted a potential "Frexit", the nationalists championed by Mrs Le Pen have made political headway in the country. Earlier in the year, Austria voted for a pro-EU president and the Netherlands a pro-EU government but with untrivial gains recorded by political parties campaigning on anti-EU platforms. Though the risks of an imminent breakup of the EU have abated with the recent election results in Austria, the Netherlands, and France, the growth of the anti-immigration and anti-EU sentiments in Europe has contributed to increased political risks in the EU.

Free flow of trade, capital, and people has enabled Singapore to enjoy good economic growth since its independence. Like many other liveable cities in the developed world, income inequality in Singapore has widened because of the congregation of globally mobile high-skill workers and high net worth investors who moved here to tap the opportunities offered by Singapore as a financial centre and a business and trading hub. Nevertheless, Singapore has managed to enjoy broad-based income growth through fiscal expenditures that supported skills training, raising productivity, and a progressive tax and transfer fiscal system that encourages employment. While the US and UK have backtracked on their global and regional integration efforts, Singapore's policies must continue to ensure that the general public continue to see the visible benefits of being connected to the rest of the world.

Although the western developed economies would continue to be important markets given their large sizes, Asian emerging economies, which enjoy good demographics and growing incomes, are expected to be the main drivers of global economic growth.[103] The member countries of the Association of South East Asian Nations (ASEAN) have been on a steadfast path of regional integration having just established the ASEAN Economic Community in 2015, and together they make up a market of more than 600 million people. ASEAN is also in the process of negotiating the Regional Comprehensive Economic Partnership, which aims to create a free trade area among the ASEAN members, and Australia, China, India, Japan, Korea, and New Zealand.

In spite of the more difficult global conditions, Singapore is fortunate to be located in the growing region of Asia. But Singapore businesses and workers must develop new marketing tools and learn new skills to tap the opportunities in the regional markets, which would have different needs and requirements than the markets in western economies. Singapore must also continue to invest in R&D, innovation, and skills training to increase its competitiveness.

We can learn from the experience of countries like Switzerland, which has continued to do well economically despite the problems in Europe. Like Singapore, Switzerland is a small and open economy. Its exports in goods and services made up more than 60% of its GDP from 2010 to 2015.[104] Manufacturing in Switzerland accounts for around 19% of the Swiss GDP over the period, well above most developed countries. This allowed Switzerland to enjoy economic growth of between 1 % and 3%, as well as relatively low unemployment rates of between 4% and 4.5% from 2010 to 2014.[105] Switzerland's achievements are built on being globally competitive by emphasising scientific research and ensuring its practical application in businesses and other areas. Like Switzerland, Singapore can do well by investing in technological and market development to serve a niche in the global market in spite of the economic headwinds. Fiscal strategies must continue to support business investments in Research, Innovation and Enterprise.

Growth is expected to be more volatile as the driver of global growth shifts from the West to Asia. China, the second largest economy in the world, which has enjoyed high growth rates based on an investment driven export-oriented strategy, is in the process of transforming its economic growth model to one driven internally by domestic consumption. The economic restructuring in China and other countries in ASEAN could be disrupted by domestic politics if the benefits from economic reforms are not well distributed within the population.

Regional growth may also be derailed by geopolitical conflicts. US President Donald Trump said during his inaugural speech on 20 January 2017 that it is the right of "all nations to put their own interests first". He had also said during his election campaign that the United States would no longer act as the policeman of the world. Though it is still too early to conclude that the US military would disengage from Asia, in the event that the US decides to do so, countries in the region may start to exert their military prowess to fill the power vacuum, and this would contribute to higher risks of military conflict that would disrupt the region's growth trajectory.

Low interest rates have contributed to over-inflated financial and property assets around the world since the Global Financial Crisis. As the US Federal Reserve embarks on monetary tightening, the adjustments to higher interest rates will add to volatilities in the financial and property asset markets around the world, which will in turn be transmitted to the real economy.

Summary

The world has become so interconnected now that shifts in governments around the world to look inward, especially in large countries such as the US and in the EU, would have profound downstream effects. Beyond reduction in international trade and investment and the risk of geopolitical conflicts, the world would become more vulnerable to transboundary issues, such as credit and financial crises, disease, cybercrime, climate change, and terrorism, which require countries to work with one another so that localised events in one part of the world do not transmit to the rest of the world and escalate into global disasters.

In this increasingly volatile world, Singapore must continue to maintain a sufficiently large war chest to buffer its businesses and workers against the caprices of the world. In addition to investing in upgrading the skills of workers and capabilities of businesses, Singapore must continue to pursue a prudent fiscal policy to ensure that its fiscal reserves are not drawn down unnecessarily so that its powder is kept dry for the next crisis that hits it.

Chapter 21

Double-Edged Sword of Technology

Technology as Enabler of Growth

Singapore's phenomenal growth as a global hub in manufacturing and services has been based on the scientific and technological advancements that made sea and air travel prevalent, as well as the internet revolution which accelerated off-shoring of economic activities, and made cross border transactions and collaboration pervasive. Singapore's industrialisation efforts have also benefited from sectors that grew on the waves of technological advances such as the development of transistors for radios and televisions, membrane technology for water desalination, and biomedical sciences for pharmaceutical production. The Singapore government recognises the impact of technology on economic growth and has ramped up its investments in the development of technology as a driver for economic growth.

Since 1991, when the first National Technology plan was launched, total (public and private) R&D expenditure has grown from around 1% of GDP to more than 2% of GDP currently. Singapore has since then developed a significant base of R&D capabilities in areas such as biomedical sciences, engineering, electronics, and marine technology. In fact, Singapore now has more R&D researchers per million people than the UK and Japan.[106] The 2014 Global Innovation Index collated by INSEAD places Singapore at seventh position globally, just below the United States and ahead of other cities in Asia. The government continues to invest in R&D to help tech start-ups develop new products. The number of start-ups in the high-tech sector has grown by 85% from 2005 to 2014.[107] In 2014, Prime Minister Lee Hsien Loong announced that Singapore would be embarking on a Smart Nation initiative to leverage on the Internet of Things, Big Data, and analytics to develop solutions and applications that addresses challenges due to urbanisation. A ministerial committee, chaired by Deputy Prime Minister Teo Chee Hean, oversees a Smart Nation and Digital Government Group formed under the Prime Minister's Office to spearhead Smart Nation projects. These developments have put Singapore in good stead to sustain growth by creating innovative, cutting edge products and services.

Disruption of Business and Employment Models

However, while technology is a growth enabler, it is also a disruptor. A 2013 study by Oxford[108] estimates that almost half of the jobs in the US are at risk of being automated in the next 20 years. A US market research firm predicted that robots will eliminate 6% of jobs in the United States by 2021.[109] Up until the 1980s, industrialisation had led to the growth of middle-skill blue-collar jobs (such as production line operations) and white-collar jobs (such as administration and sales) which arose from the organisation of jobs based on division of labour. Post 1980s, technological-driven computerisation has eliminated the routine manual as well as administrative tasks found in many middle-skill positions while low-skill jobs in the service sector, such as in food processing and cleaning, remain because they tend to be non-routine and difficult to automate. On the other end, demand for high-skill professional jobs, such as programming, designing, engineering, and management, with the skills to complement automation and computerisation has grown.[110] With advancements in computing technology, such as the development of "Artificial Intelligence" and

"Deep Learning", even tasks involved in professional jobs that require tacit knowledge, such as financial analysis, legal advice, and medical diagnosis, could be computerised. Moving forward, the jobs that are expected to remain in demand would require abstract thinking, creativity, and personalised service, which complement and interface with the computerisation of the future.

The internet has enabled people to trade goods and services directly with one another, but this has also disrupted traditional businesses and employment models. For example, platforms such as Uber has allowed private owners of cars to provide rides for a fee, essentially an alternative mode of transport competing with taxis. Similarly, Airbnb allows property owners to rent out their homes for short stays, offering holiday makers and business travellers alternatives to hotels. Increasingly, people are taking up "gigs" via the internet by offering their free time to run errands such as making deliveries or even providing professional services like editing or graphic design. Businesses are taking advantage of such developments to outsource work to contract workers and even to crowdsource for services and ideas. The creation of such "sharing" or "gig" economies provide opportunities for new businesses to emerge, but it also causes disruptions to traditional businesses and drives shifts in the relationship between workers and employers. Under the new models, employers have become more like contractors who engage the workers, low skill as well as medium skill, as freelancers or contract workers for "gigs".

Technology will continue to bring about disruptions to businesses as well as workers. Singapore has no choice but to continue investing in technology to drive productivity improvements for sustained growth. In Budget 2016, the government announced a $4.5 billion Industry Transformation Programme on top of the $19 billion 5-year Research, Innovation and Enterprise plan announced in 2015. Through the Industry Transformation Programme, the government will provide support for transformation at the enterprise and industry levels through the adoption and deployment of technology, scaling up for efficiencies, creation of new products and processes, and development of new overseas markets. This was followed up with a

$2.4 billion package announced in Budget 2017 to help businesses strengthen capabilities through digitalisation, innovation, and scaling up globally in line with the recommendations of the Committee on the Future Economy.

Increased Vulnerability of Workers

With advances in technology, new jobs created would comprise mainly low-skill ones on one end and highly paid skilled professions on the other end, while more jobs in the broad middle jobs would be automated. In addition, the low-skill jobs are likely to be gigs that provide neither work security nor opportunities for skill development and are mostly at risk of being automated. Singapore must ensure that its workers move up to fill high-skill jobs in the new economy, rather than fall into the low-skill spectrum or become structurally unemployed.

According to a study by the Ministry of Manpower (MOM),[111] the global shocks in the last decade from 2004 to 2015 displaced between 8,500 and 15,580 workers every year over the period. Among those retrenched in 2015, 66% who were made redundant in the first 9 months of the year re-entered into employment by December 2015, less than the 68% the year before. Eight out of ten did so in about 3 months or less, mostly in a different industry. According to the MOM study, those aged 40 and above formed the majority (65%) of resident workers retrenched in 2015. In addition, PMETs have been more at risk of redundancy than other occupational groups since 2012 and their re-entry to the workforce is also lower.

Our workforce continues to age and the share of PMETs in the workforce is expected to grow from the current 54 per cent to about two-thirds in 2030.

We can therefore expect more workers to be displaced more frequently as technological advancements and globalisation continue to accelerate. The displaced workers would also find it more difficult and take longer to find re-employment. The longer the workers stay unemployed, the more their skills and experience deteriorate and the less employable they become. The group of lower-skill workers could grow, and incomes could become more polarised over time.

Based on a survey undertaken by the MOM in 2016,[112] there were 167,000 "primary" freelancers, i.e., workers who do freelancing as their main job. The proportion of freelancers in the workforce has been flat within the range of 8–10% of employed residents in the past 10 years. Including "secondary" freelancers, who freelance as part-timers in addition to holding a primary job, Singapore has a total number of around 200,000 freelancers. The number of freelancers in the Singapore workforce is significantly lower than the 20–30% of the workforce who engage in freelance work in the United States and the EU-15, according to a 2016 study by the McKinsey Global Institute.[113] In addition, about 81% of freelancers in Singapore do so as a preferred choice because of the consequent independence, autonomy, and flexibility. This is higher than the 70% in the McKinsey study. The differences between the Singapore survey and the McKinsey survey could perhaps be attributed to the fact that there are more opportunities for formal employment in Singapore. Singapore's unemployment is also significantly lower. The finding that is common to both surveys is that freelancers using online work platforms like Uber and Deliveroo were the minority, comprising 5–6% of those who engage in freelance work. Nevertheless, both the Singapore government and McKinsey suggested that the freelance workforce would grow as the unemployed population and demand for independent services from both consumers and organisations grow. Consequently, the workforce would become more vulnerable as freelancers grapple with issues regarding income security, access to credit, pension savings, training and credentials, etc.

Government Response

In response to these trends, the government has been increasing its expenditures in Continuing Education and Training to enable the workforce to cope with the continual job disruptions and employment shifts. For vulnerable low-skill workers, the government provides subsidies to help them stay in formal employment and continue to upgrade and stay employable through the workfare income supplement and training schemes. If the workforce were to become more polarised, workfare would require much higher outlays.

The government has also been reviewing and enhancing the education system[114] and is rolling out the SkillsFuture initiative to help prepare its people for the new economy and enable workers to continue learning and relearning though their working lives to stay relevant and fill good jobs created in the new economy.

To help displaced workers move to new industries, the government has launched specific schemes such as the Career Support Programme in 2015, which provide wage support for up to 1 year to employers who employ displaced mature workers above 40 years old in mid-level jobs. This complements various Place and Train and Professional Conversion programs, which provide subsidies for employers in sectors where there are labour shortages, to put in place structured programmes for recruitment, retraining, and retention of workers displaced from other sectors. Through the ComCare Short-to-Medium Term Assistance programme, low-income workers who are displaced can apply for financial assistance to assist with family expenses while they look for new jobs. Services such as career counselling, employer networking, training advisory, and a jobs database are also provided by the government to reduce the informational gaps and help displaced workers access job opportunities. These schemes are being expanded as the pace of disruption due to technological advancement picks up.

The government is also keeping a close watch on the number of freelancers in the workforce. On 6 March 2017, the government announced in parliament that a tripartite workgroup (comprising the government, employers, and unions) would be formed to study and address the concerns of freelancers and come up with workable solutions for the well-being of the freelancing workforce.

The Fundamental Challenge

Thus far, the government policy has been to help people who help themselves. As Deputy Prime Minister Tharman Shanmugaratnam put it while speaking at the St Gallen Symposium in 2015, "If you provide help for someone who is willing to study hard; if you provide help for someone who is willing to take up a job and work at it, and make life not so easy if you stay out of work; if you provide help for someone who wants to own a home…it transforms culture." It is this culture of self-reliance that has enabled Singapore to succeed while maintaining relatively low government spending and revenues.

The key challenge in the future would be in maintaining this culture of self-reliance. Technological advancements will make it increasingly difficult for a broad majority of Singaporeans to stay in middle-income jobs. While the government faces increasing pressure to play a larger role to help a more vulnerable workforce, it must be careful that it does not do so in a way that weakens the self-reliance of the people.

Chapter 22

Self-Reliance

There are three distinct but interrelated features of Singapore's fiscal strategies that are most noteworthy. First, the strategies contribute to macroeconomic stability with the building up of budget surpluses, which support a strong and stable Singapore dollar and buffer businesses and workers against global shocks. Second, the fiscal policies marshal resources for sustainable economic growth by creating a low-tax environment that attracts investments, optimising land use, developing efficient infrastructures, and promoting the development of skills in the workforce. Finally, the policies ensure that the people enjoy broad-based benefits and visible improvements in their lives. These make up the three planks of Singapore's fiscal strategies, which must work hand-in-hand for the strategies to be sustainable.

But each of the three elements are diametrically opposed to one or the other. For example, fiscal policies driven solely by providing benefits for the people would be sustainable only with high taxes, but that would then deter investment in Singapore's small and open economy. Keeping taxes low while providing fiscal benefits to satisfactorily address the inexhaustible needs of the people would lead to unsustainable fiscal deficits that result in macroinstability. The three elements are an impossible trinity unless they are held together by the culture of self-reliance as shown in Fig. 13.

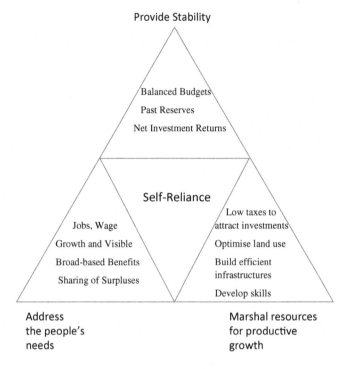

Figure 13:   Framework for Sustainable Fiscal Strategies.

Under this model, a minimalist welfare system provided by a small and lean government is made possible because a self-reliant citizenry does not depend on fiscal subsidies and handouts. The resulting low taxes and balanced budgets create the benign investment climate that supports economic growth and generates employment to help Singaporeans stay self-reliant. Besides good land planning and efficient infrastructure, economic growth is sustained by a hard-working and self-reliant labour force that is motivated to upgrade and reskill as the economy restructures.

Fiscal Interventions to Support Self-Reliance

Singapore's fiscal strategies have been underpinned by self-reliance since independence. From the 1960s, low taxes coupled with fiscal incentives have served to promote investments that create jobs to reduce unemployment in Singapore. The government maintained the CPF system set up by the British in 1955 to enable employees to save for their retirement needs. The system was expanded to enable the employees to also fund their medical and housing expenditures from the savings. In the 1970s, the government developed institutions such as the National Wage Council which helped ensure that the wages of workers grow while ensuring that the economy remains competitive. These measures enabled the broad majority of Singaporeans to provide for themselves and their families with minimal fiscal support except in the specific areas of housing, healthcare, and education.

In recent years, the government has had to provide additional fiscal support to help workers remain self-reliant in an environment where workers are increasingly vulnerable. From 2007, the government implemented the WIS scheme to encourage employers to employ low-skill workers. Additional measures were introduced to help older workers stay employed through the Special Employment Credit (SEC) scheme introduced in 2011. Through the Productivity and Innovation Credit (PIC) introduced in 2010, businesses were given generous fiscal incentives to invest in productivity improvements. They are then encouraged through the WCS introduced in 2013 to share the fruits of productivity gains by raising the wages of employees. The Progressive Wage System (PWS) implemented in 2014 enables workers in selected sectors to earn higher salaries by raising productivity through skills training. These bold and innovative measures are intended to help businesses cope with higher costs as the economy restructures. To ensure fiscal sustainability, the broad-based PIC, SEC, and WCS are temporary schemes that would be phased out and replaced by permanent but targeted measures under the SkillsFuture initiative that would enable Singapore workers to continually meet the emerging challenges brought about by globalisation and technological advances and help businesses become more competitive.

Besides fiscal support to help vulnerable low-skill workers stay employed, social spending would also come under increasing upward pressures, especially in healthcare and support for the elderly and an ageing population. At the same time, economic spending on R&D and education expenditures to help businesses and workers keep pace with technological advances and shifts in global demand must be maintained, if not increased. Over the shorter term, spending on infrastructure development is also needed to ensure that Singapore continues to be a liveable and vibrant city for the benefit of its people as well as to ensure that the city state stays attractive to global talent and investors. Nevertheless, the government has managed to live within its means.

Room for More — But There is a Limit

There is still space to manoeuvre within the government's fiscal strategies framework to finance the growing needs sustainably, though it would be increasingly difficult to do so. The government could look into tapping more on the NII to fund the spending increases without losing tax competitiveness. Currently, up to 50% of the expected long-term rate of return on the reserves could be taken into the budget for spending. The government has some headroom to tweak the formula to take in a larger share of the investment returns from reserves, without effectively drawing down on the reserves, but the trade-off is a slower rate of growth of the reserves.

Income taxes in Singapore are still among the lowest in the world,[115] and the government can afford to raise them if need be, but such tax increases will be limited by the need to stay competitive. The GST can also be raised, but it will have to be offset by even more transfers to the lower income to offset the regressive impact of the tax. Besides raising income taxes, the government could also raise indirect taxes such as taxes on luxury cars and larger homes as it did in Budget 2013 to make the tax system more progressive. However, there is a social limit to how much the rich could be taxed to increase transfers to the rest of society. The emphasis on meritocracy and self-reliance over the years had made it very natural for high-wage workers and high-net-worth individuals to think that their achievements are due to their own hard work and abilities and resent the payment of taxes to subsidise lower-income households. In fact, concerns have been raised several times in the parliament that increasing taxes at the top end to finance more transfers to the bottom end would risk creating a "crutch mentality" among the lower income and undermine the spirit of hard work and self-reliance that has been nurtured over the years.[116]

The Need to Manage Shift in Values

While the increase in healthcare spending for the aged and investments in R&D, infrastructure development and education could be planned ahead of time and managed within the framework of fiscal sustainability — the government has a good track record of doing so — the demand for increased social spending would be the most difficult to manage because of the underlying shift in social values that it entails.

First, population ageing translates to a larger number of elderly who have more difficulties coping with the economic and social changes brought about by technological advances. The ageing population would be less supportive of painful restructuring measures that yield economic growth over the longer term and are likely to benefit younger people. On the other hand, demands for elderly support in various forms would grow. The government must ensure that sufficient fiscal resources are set aside to invest in future generations while meeting the needs of the elderly.

Second, as the wage gap widens due to polarisation of the workforce, there would be greater demands for increased fiscal support for low-wage and vulnerable workers. The government would be expected to enlarge the safety net for the workforce when more workers become more vulnerable to displacements by globalisation and technology. The increasing rates of economic disruptions and skills obsolescence, coupled with higher life expectancies, would make it more and more difficult for larger groups of workers — low-income ones as well as those in the middle-income group — to stay in jobs and be self-reliant without additional help. In that event, the government must not heed pressures to expand fiscal transfers to the broad majority of workers, which would have to be funded by higher taxes, and risk feeding a "crutch" mentality. Rather, the government should continue to focus on non-income support to help vulnerable workers develop the skills that would be in demand in the new economy.

Third, social discomfort over visible disparities in incomes and wealth have grown. There are more voices calling for measures to bridge the income and wealth gaps, including a national minimum wage policy, higher taxes on the rich and more transfers to the poor, and drawing more on past reserves. The government has to respond to these concerns. But rather than expanding tax-and-transfer programmes that would eventually erode Singapore's ability to compete globally, Singapore must ensure that economic growth benefits Singaporeans in the broad middle- and lower-income groups by continuing with policies to intervene surgically to provide targeted support for workers, not only for low-skill workers but also for the increasingly vulnerable middle-skill workers, to stay employed in good jobs and remain economically relevant through lifelong education and upskilling.

In summary, the government must continue to create the environment for workers and businesses to do well by being globally competitive. While the government enlarges its social support for an ageing population and a more vulnerable workforce, it would have to do so carefully so that it does not inculcate a sense of entitlement and reliance by the people. An overreliance on the state for social support would result in higher government expenditures that would make it more difficult to continue its prudent fiscal policies, which have been important to the maintenance of investor confidence in a small open economy. If the government is perceived to be compromising on its fiscal strategies of prudence and drawing down on the reserves in an unsustainable manner, businesses would doubt Singapore's ability to support the development of globally competitive companies and workers and maintain macroeconomic stability. The loss of confidence could translate to withdrawal of investments and send Singapore down an unsustainable spiral of lower or negative growth. That is why, in the Budget Statement delivered in February 2017, the Minister for Finance Mr Heng Swee Keat announced a permanent 2% cut to the budget caps of all ministries and organs of state from 2017 onwards. He also hinted that the government would raise revenues through new taxes and higher taxes to ensure that "our future generations remain on a sustainable fiscal footing." All these signify the government's resolve to prioritise its spending needs and live within its means to maintain investor confidence in the nation.

Self-Reliance and Singapore's Success

While most economists have highlighted the importance of capital, technology, and development of political and economic institutions to economic development, there are also others who as far back as the early 1900s[117] were of the view that social attitudes and values are the decisive determinants of which economies would succeed and which would fail. This view has been reiterated recently by some academics who suggested that the success of national economies was driven by cultural factors such as hard work, belief in the importance of individual effort, trust, and honesty.[118]

Since Singapore separated from Malaysia to become a sovereign nation, journalists and academics have predicted that the small city state would not succeed. In fact, Singapore's constraints were described in the 1986 Economic Committee Report which pointed out that Singapore does not have a domestic market or hinterland and "if all factors are merely equal, Singapore will not be an ideal place to locate a business. We are far away from export markets and susceptible to trade disruptions". Indeed, Singapore's current achievements defy conventional economic theory if one disregards the impact of culture of self-reliance. But Singapore's policies since independence has been based on helping every member of the society take individual responsibility for taking care of himself and his family and to contribute to society. This provided the motivation for the population to work hard, upgrade their skills, and innovate and enabled Singapore to continually reinvent itself and compensate for its disadvantages by offering businesses a more conducive business environment and a better chance to do well and earn a higher rate of return than in other comparable countries.

In my view, the best description of the importance of self-reliance to Singapore's success was made by Deputy Prime Minister Tharman when he spoke at the St Gallen Symposium in 2015. In response to an interviewer's question, Mr Tharman said that the one thing that has been paramount behind Singapore's rise is "an attitude of mind". He elaborated that Singapore "took advantage of disadvantage" and "converted permanent disadvantage into continuing advantage", referring to the city state's constraints as a small nation with virtually neither a domestic market nor natural resources and comprising "a diverse group of people of different origins who were willing to work hard and had to fend for themselves and make themselves relevant to the world." He pointed out that in western societies, the "traditional concepts of welfare and social expenditure and government intervention have led to a weakening of private initiative and personal responsibility." On the other hand, with reference to the social compact that Singapore was trying to achieve, he said that "an active government can intervene to support social mobility to develop opportunities and to take care of the old, but not undermine personal and family responsibility." Using the home ownership scheme as an example, Mr Tharman said that "It's about keeping alive a culture where I feel proud that I own my home and I earn my own success through my job. I feel proud that I'm raising my own family. Keeping that culture going is what keeps the society vibrant."

It would have been a very different story for Singapore had the government adopted a policy of providing social assistance for unemployment and making public services such as medical services and housing freely available from the start. The resultant high social spending would have to be offset by high taxes, which would deter business investments. Individuals would also not see the point in working if they had to pay high taxes to subsidise those who were unemployed, especially given the diversity in the population — the newly created nation being made up of immigrants from China, India, and the neighbouring countries. In the 1960s, when unemployment was high and growing, the new citizens would have preferred to stay unemployed so that they could enjoy generous unemployment benefits and social services provided by their newly adopted nation. Inadvertently, the lack of investments and low employment growth would make it difficult for the government to raise revenues to sustain the high levels of subsidies for public services and social transfers, leading to budget deficits. Over time, debts would be incurred to fund the unsustainable budget deficits, which would lead to depreciation of the Singapore dollar and higher imported inflation. The government would not be able to keep borrowing and at some point, lenders would stop lending or only do so at higher interest rates. The government would have no choice but to introduce painful tax increases and reduce or withdraw the expenditures on public services and social transfers. Singapore would have been trapped in a cycle of high taxes, low investment, and low growth and remained a Third World country.

At the 2015 St Gallen Symposium, Deputy Prime Minister Tharman used the metaphor of a trampoline to describe what social safety nets should aim to achieve. Like trampolines, social safety nets should help people bounce back up. I think this offers an insight into Singapore's fiscal strategies to tackle the challenges ahead. First and foremost, fiscal resources would continue supporting economic growth to create jobs and opportunities for the people. This would generate the resources to help those who are able to help themselves. For those who might be dislocated in the process of restructuring, fiscal policies should enable them to bounce back up by investing in new skills needed for new jobs. They could then continue to contribute to growth and in turn give back to others who need help.

At the centre of this virtuous cycle lies self-reliance. The constitutional requirement for the Singapore government to live within its means is in itself established on the idea of self-reliance at the national level. Fiscal policies would have to continue to adapt to

Singapore's changing needs — tax rates and tax structures would change, and the reserves may be used in more ways to meet increasing and new needs — but ultimately, fiscal policies must also entrench the culture of self-reliance within the people by giving individuals who put in the effort a better opportunity to achieve progress as the economy restructures and grow. Though the government can and should provide help where it can, it must also allow businesses to fail and workers to lose their jobs when they are no longer competitive. The government can provide the necessary infrastructure for resources to be redirected to new growth areas, but businesses and workers must also be continually spurred to adapt and grow in response to economic, technological, and geopolitical changes in the world, painful as it may be. There is probably no other way for a small island like Singapore — a piece of granite rock with no hinterland and little natural resources — in its journey towards sustained progress and prosperity.

Notes

1. Statistics compiled by Hui Ying SNG in "Singapore's 50 years of Socioeconomic Transformation: Notes and Quick Facts" from *Singapore 2065: Leading Insights on Economy and Environment from 50 Singapore Icons and Beyond* (World Scientific, 2016).
2. *Singapore in Figures 2016*, Singapore Department of Statistics.
3. Lee Soon Ann, Chapter 2, *Singapore's Economic Development: Retrospection and Reflections* (World Scientific, 2016).
4. 1967 Annual Budget Statement.
5. 1959 Annual Budget Statement.
6. Prime Minister Lee Hsien Loong's Eulogy for Dr Goh Keng Swee.
7. Kin W Chin, *The Defence of Malaysia and Singapore: The Transformation of a Security System 1957–1971* (Cambridge University Press, 1983).
8. *Financing a City: Developing Foundations for Sustainable Growth* (Centre for Liveable Cities, 2014).
9. Economic Planning Unit, 1964, p. 2.
10. Ichiro Sugimoto and Eu Chye Tan, "Government Fiscal Behavior and Economic Growth of Singapore in the Twentieth Century", *The Singapore Economic Review*, Vol. 56, No. 1 (2011), pp. 19–40 (© World Scientific Publishing Company).
11. 1959 Annual Budget Statement.
12. Lee Soon Ann, Chapter 2, *Singapore's Economic Development: Retrospection and Reflections* (World Scientific, 2016).
13. Speech by Dr Goh Keng Swee at the *Financial Times* conference in London on 21 November 1972.

14. Statistics compiled by Hui Ying SNG in "Singapore's 50 years of Socioeconomic Transformation: Notes and Quick Facts" from *Singapore 2065: Leading Insights on Economy and Environment from 50 Singapore Icons and Beyond* (World Scientific, 2016).
15. 1968 Annual Budget Statement.
16. Speech by Dr Goh Keng Swee at the *Financial Times* conference in London on 21 November 1972.
17. Lee Soon Ann, Chapter 2, *Singapore's Economic Development: Retrospection and Reflections* (World Scientific, 2016).
18. Speech by Dr Goh Keng Swee at the Financial Times conference in London on 21 November 1972.
19. "The Singapore Economy: New Directions". Report of the Economic Committee (Ministry of Trade and Industry, 1986).
20. "The Strategic Economic Plan: Towards a Developed Nation". Report of the Economic Planning Committee (Ministry of Trade and Industry, 1991).
21. "New Challenges, Fresh Goals: Towards a Dynamic Global City". Report of the Economic Review Committee (Ministry of Trade and Industry, 2003).
22. "Highly Skilled People, Innovative Economy, Distinctive Global City". Report of the Economic Strategies Committee (2010).
23. "Projected GDP per capita ranking", 5 June 2015, accessed on 16 December 2016, http://statisticstimes.com/economy/projected-world-gdp-capita-ranking.phpIMF World Economic Outlook Database, April 2015.
24. Choy Keen Meng, "Studies on the Singapore Economy" (World Scientific, 2012).
25. Leslie Shaffer "Singapore's growth miss may be the canary in the coalmine", CNBC.com, 13 October 16, accessed on 15 December 2016.
26. Tan Kim Song and Manu Bhaskaran, Chapter 4, Singapore's Economic *Development — Retrospection and Reflections* (World Scientific, 2016).
27. "Budget Highlights Financial Year 2009; Box 3.2: Fiscal Multipliers in Singapore" (Ministry of Finance, 2009).
28. Speech by Mr Ravi Menon, Managing Director of the Monetary Authority of Singapore, at the Asian Bureau of Financial and Economic Research (ABFER) Opening Gala Dinner, Singapore, 21 May 2013.

29. Feature article "Update on the Value Added from Singapore's Exports", Economic Survey of Singapore, third quarter, 2012.
30. "124,500 Workers Sign Up for SPUR in Just Six Months", Ministry of Manpower Media Release, 3 July 2009.
31. Izumi Ohno and Daniel Kitaw "Kaizen National Movement: A Study of Quality and Productivity Improvement in Asia and Africa" (Japan International Cooperation Agency (JICA) and GRIPS Development Forum , 2011)
32. Huff, W. G., *The Economic Growth of Singapore — Trade and Development in the Twentieth Century* (Cambridge University Press, 1994).
33. Budget highlights, various years.
34. Keynote addresses by Mr Lee Kuan Yew, Chairman of GIC at the GIC 25th and 35th anniversary dinners.
35. Speech by President Tony Tan at Temasek Holdings 40th anniversary dinner
36. Temasek Factsheet: http://www.temasek.com.sg/investorrelations/investorlibrary/investorfactsheet.
37. Address by Mr Tharman Shanmugaratnam, Deputy Prime Minister, and Minister for Finance at the Temasek 39th anniversary dinner.
38. Budget highlights, financial year 2012 (Ministry of Finance, 2012).
39. Budget Highlights, financial year 2016 (Ministry of Finance, 2016).
40. GIC Annual Report 2016.
41. Marissa Lee, "Expect period of lower growth, warns DPM Tharman", *Straits Times*, 29 September 2016.
42. "Total Estimated Receipts by Object Class" for financial years from 2014 to 2016 (Ministry of Finance, 2014–2016).
43. Analysis of Revenue and Expenditure — Financial Year 2017 (Ministry of Finance, 20 February 2017).
44. Statement of Assets and Liabilities as at 31 March 2016 (Ministry of Finance, 2016).
45. Annual Report of the Maritime Port Authority of Singapore for Financial Year ended 31 December 2015.
46. Statement of Assets and Liabilities as at 31 March 2016 (Ministry of Finance, 2016).
47. Analysis of Revenue and Expenditure — Financial Year 2017 (Ministry of Finance, 20 February 2017).

48. Analysis of Revenue and Expenditure — Financial Year 2017 (Ministry of Finance, 20 February 2017).
49. "Are Operating Revenues Growing with GDP?" Feature article, Budget Highlights — Financial Year 2006 (Ministry of Finance, 2006).
50. "Discretionary Fiscal Policy in Economic Downturns", feature article, 2009 Budget.
51. Budget Highlights — Financial Years 2005 to 2016.
52. Christian Aspalter, *Discovering the Welfare State in East Asia* (Westport: Praeger, 2002); Goodman, R., White, G. and Kwon, H., "East Asian Social Policy: A Model to Emulate?" (*Social Policy Review*, Vol. 9. Social Policy Association, London, pp. 359–380, 1997).
53. David Jacobs, "Low public expenditures on social welfare: do East Asian countries have a secret?" (*International Journal of Social Welfare*, Vol. 9, Issue 1, 2000).
54. Speech by Prime Minister and Minister for Finance Lee Hsien Loong at the Launch of Comcare on 28 June 2005.
55. Phang, Sock Yong and KIM, Kyunghwan. "Singapore's Housing Policies: 1960–2013. Frontiers in Development Policy: Innovative Development" (Case Studies. 123–153. Research Collection School of Economics, 2011).
56. Hugh T. W. Tan, L. M. Chou, Darren C. J. Yeo and Peter K. L. Ng, "The Natural Heritage of Singapore" Table 4.1 (Prentice Hall-Pearson Education, 2010)
57. Data from Singapore Department of Statistics.
58. JTC annual reports (2008 and 2011).
59. Statistics compiled by Hui Ying SNG in "Singapore's 50 years of Socioeconomic Transformation: Notes and Quick Facts" from *Singapore 2065 — Leading Insights on Economy and Environment from 50 Singapore Icons and Beyond* (World Scientific, 2016).
60. Matt Yardley, "Developing successful Public-Private Partnerships to foster investment in universal broadband networks" (Analysys Mason, 2012).
61. Lee Soon Ann, Chapter 2, *Singapore's Economic Development — Retrospection and Reflections* (World Scientific, 2016).
62. By Brenda S. A. Yeoh, "Singapore: Hungry for Foreign Workers at All Skill Levels", *Migration Information Source*, the online journal of the Migration Policy Institute, 1 January 2007, accessed on 22 January 2017, http://www.migrationpolicy.org/article/singapore-hungry-foreign-workers-all-skill-levels.

63. Md Mizanur Rahman, "Foreign Manpower in Singapore: Classes, Policies and Management" (February 2006, Asia Research Institute, National University of Singapore, Working Paper Series No. 57).
64. "Employment Trend and Structure", report (Manpower Research and Statistics Department, May 2004).
65. "Redundancy and Re-entry into Employment 2015", report (Manpower Research and Statistics Department, April 2016).
66. Lim Chong Yah, *Singapore's National Wages Council: An Insider's View* (World Scientific, 2013).
67. "Labour Force in Singapore 2015", report (Ministry of Manpower, 2015).
68. Manu Bhaskaran, Ho Seng Chee, Donald Low, Tan Kim Song, Sudhir Vadaketh, Yeok Lam Keong, "Inequality and the Need for a New Social Compact" (background paper for *Singapore Perspectives 2012*).
69. Speech by Prime Minister and Minister for Finance Lee Hsien Loong at the debate of the Annual Budget in parliament on 1 March 2006.
70. Annual Budget Statement 2015.
71. Table 3: Tax Burden in Selected Economies, Income Growth, Inequality and Mobility Trends in Singapore, MoF occasional paper, August 2015.
72. "Ministry for Finance Occasional Paper on Income Growth, Inequality and Mobility Trends in Singapore" (Ministry of Finance, 2015).
73. Speech by Minister for Health Mr Yong Nyuk Lin at the World Health Organisation Seminar in Singapore in 1967.
74. 1968 Budget speech.
75. Belinda Yuen, "Squatters No More: Singapore Social Housing" (*Global Urban Development Magazine*, Vol. 3, Issue 1, November 2007).
76. Phang, Sock Yong and KIM, Kyunghwan. "Singapore's Housing Policies: 1960–2013. Frontiers in Development Policy: Innovative Development" (Case Studies. 123–153. Research Collection School Of Economics, 2011).
77. Statement released by Ministry of National Development on 21 April 2012.
78. More Housing Improvement Programme (HIP) Projects by 2012 (Housing and Development Board, 3 March 2011).

78. Report on the Audit of the Financial Statements of the Housing and Development Board for the Year Ended 31st March 2016 (Government Gazette, 16 September 2016).
80. Goh Chor Boon, S. Gopinathan, "The Development of Education in Singapore since 1965: Background paper prepared for the Asia Education Study Tour for African Policy Makers, June 18–30, 2006" (National Institute of Education, Nanyang Technological University, Singapore).
81. Goh Keng Swee, *Socialism that Works — the Singapore Way* (Singapore, 1976).
82. Speech by Dr Goh Keng Swee at the *Financial Times* conference in London on 21 November 1972.
83. Ichiro Sugimoto and Eu Chye Tan, "Government Fiscal Behavior and Economic Growth of Singapore in the Twentieth Century", the *Singapore Economic Review*, Vol. 56, Issue 1 (2011).
84. UNESCO Institute for Statistics.
85. William A. Haseltine, *Affordable Excellence: The Singapore Healthcare Story: How to Create and Manage Sustainable Healthcare Systems* (Ridge Books, 2013).
86. Lim Meng Kin "Health Care System in Transition II. Singapore Part I. An Overview of Health Care Systems in Singapore," *Journal of Public Health Medicine* Vol. 20, Issue 1 (1998).
87. Ajay Tandon, Christopher JL Murray, Jeremy A Lauer, David B Evans "Measuring Overall Health System Performance for 191 Countries" (GPE Discussion Paper Series: No. 30, EIP/GPE/EQC World Health Organization).
88. Budget documents (2007 and 2017).
89. Addendum to the President's Opening Address to the 13th Parliament (2016).
90. Budget documents (2007 and 2017).
91. Budget Highlights (2009 and 2012).
92. 2006 Annual Budget Statement.
93. 2011 Annual Budget Statement.
94. *Pensions at a Glance: Asia-Pacific Edition* (World Bank and OECD, 2010).
95. Annex B-1 to Budget speech 2015.
96. "A Sustainable Population for a Dynamic Singapore — Population White Paper 2013" (The National Population and Talent Division, January 2013).

97. Recommendations of the Tripartite Committee on Employability of Older Workers (2005).

98. Laurence Chandy, Geoffrey Gertz, "With Little Notice, Globalization Reduced Poverty" (YaleGlobal, 5 July 2011).

99. Lawrence Mishel and Teresa Kroeger, "Superb income growth in 2015 nearly single-handedly restored incomes lost in the Great Recession", 13 September 2016, accessed on 14 December 2016, http://www. epi.org/blog/superb-income-growth-in-2015-nearly-single-handedly-restored-incomes-lost-in-the-great-recession/.

100. Elise Gould, "Wage inequality continued its 35-year rise in 2015", Economic Policy Institute, 10 March 2016, EPI Briefing Paper #421.

101. "Ford Cancels a $1.6 Billion Mexico Plant and Adds 700 Jobs in Michigan", *Reuters*, updated: 4 January 2017, accessed on 5 January 2017, http://fortune.com/2017/01/03/ford-cancels-mexico-plant-trump/.

102. Rowena Mason, "How did UK end up voting to leave the European Union", *The Guardian*, 24 June 2016, accessed on 14 December 2016 https://www.theguardian.com/politics/2016/jun/24/how-did-uk-end-up-voting-leave-european-union.

103. "Growth Drivers in Asia and Singapore" — Opening Remarks by Mr Heng Swee Keat, Minister for Finance, at the UBS Wealth Insights Conference on 12th Jan 2016.

104. World Bank national accounts data and OECD National Accounts data files.

105. International Labour Organization, Key Indicators of the Labour Market database.

106. United Nations Educational, Scientific and Cultural Organization (UNESCO) Institute for Statistics data.

107. Opening remarks by President Tony Tan at MIT Global Innovation Gala Dinner on 21 July 2015.

108. Michael A. Osborne and Carl Benedict Frey, *The Future of Employment: How Susceptible Are Jobs to Computerisation?* (Oxford, 2013).

109. Olivia Solon, "Robots will eliminate 6% of all US jobs by 2021, report says", *The Guardian*, 14 September 2016, https://www.theguardian.com/technology/2016/sep/13/artificial-intelligence-robots-threat-jobs-forrester-report.

110. Claudia Goldin, Lawrence F. Katz "Long-Run Changes in the U.S. Wage Structure: Narrowing, Widening, Polarizing" (Working Paper 13568 http://www.nber.org/papers/w13568, November 2007).

111. "Redundancy and Re-entry into Employment 2015" released in April 2016 by the Ministry of Manpower, Manpower Research and Statistics Department.

112. Speech on CPF and gig economy by Mr Lim Swee Say, Minister for Manpower at Committee of Supply 2017, 6 March 2017.

113. "Independent work: Choice, necessity, and the gig economy", report, McKinsey Global Institute, October 2016.

114. Lim Yang Liang, "Equip Students with Skills to Create Future Tech: PM" (*Straits Times*, 25 November 2014).

115. Rina Chandran, "Singapore still has low taxes, even when it's charging the rich more", Bloomberg.com, 24 February 2015, accessed on 9 December 2016, https://www.bloomberg.com/news/articles/2015-02-24/low-tax-status-intact-even-with-increase-for-wealthy.

116. Member of Parliament for Moulmein-Kallang Mr Edwin Tong Chun Fai, (Debate on Annual Budget Statement, 17 February 2012); Nominated Member of Parliament Asst Prof Tan Kheng Boon Eugene, (Debate on Annual Budget Statement, 25 February 2013); Member of Parliament for Sembawang Ms Ellen Lee (Debate on the President's Address, 8 November 2006).

117. Max Weber, *The Protestant Ethic and the Spirit of Capitalism* (1905).

118. David Landes, *The Wealth and Poverty of Nations: Why Some are So Rich and Some So Poor* (New York: W.W. Norton, 1998); Guido Tabellini, "Culture and Institutions: Economic Development in the Regions of Europe" (*Journal of the European Economic Association*, Vol. 8, Issue 4, Pages 677–716, June 2010).